William Shakespeare

THE FIRST PART OF
KING HENRY THE FOURTH

RI → HIV
full poetry → some prose
serious → commical (decret)
challengers (now) helped him to power in RI

court world (sc1) → tavern world (sc2) → rebel world (sc3)
⌐all three predicated on theft
⌐crowns: the crown, coins, cracked crown (illegitimate coin)(broken head-fighting)

William Shakespeare

THE FIRST PART OF
KING HENRY THE FOURTH

Editor
Samuel Crowl
Ohio University

TABLE OF CONTENTS

Publisher's Note

George Lyman Kittredge's insightful editions of Shakespeare have endured in part because of his eclecticism, his diversity of interests, and his wide-ranging accomplishments — all of which are reflected in the valuable notes in each volume. The plays in the *New Kittredge Shakespeare* series retain the original Kittredge notes and introductions, changed or augmented only when some modernization seems necessary. These new editions also include introductory essays by contemporary editors, notes on the plays as they have been performed on stage and film, and additional student materials.

These plays are being made available by Focus Publishing with the permission of the Kittredge heirs.

Ron Pullins, Publisher
Newburyport, 2007

Acknowledgments

I would like to thanks James H. Lake for graciously insisting that I undertake this happy project and Ron Pullins, Linda Diering, and Hailey Klein of Focus Publishing for help at every stage of the project's development including the search for an appropriate image for the cover.

Susan Crowl put her long experience of editing Robert Browning's poems to good use with winning suggestions about how to edit Kittredge's text and notes and suggested several new glosses. I would like to thank Douglas Campbell (Falstaff), Douglas Rain (Hal), and the late Jason Robards, Jr. (Hotspur) for first introducing me to this play in their wonderful production at Stratford, Canada in the summer of 1958. I was seventeen and can still remember details of their vital work fifty years later. Thanks also to Orson Welles, John Woodvine, Kevin Kline, and Michael Gambon for creating memorable Falstaffs in more recent years on stage and screen.

This edition is for Emerson Kelleher Crowl who joins a great crew of "nimble-footed madcaps" who are my youthful companions: Charlie, Aidan, Theo, Audrey, and Miles.

Samuel Crowl
2009

INTRODUCTION TO THE KITTREDGE EDITION

HENRY THE FOURTH, PART ONE was entered in the Stationers' Register on February 25, 1598, by Andrew Wyse, as "The historye of Henry the IIIIth with his battaile of Shrewsburye against Henry Hottspurre of the Northe with the conceipted mirthe of Sir John Falstoff," and the First Quarto came out in the same year. Seven other Quartos of *Part I* appeared from 1599 to 1639. The printer of the First Folio (1623) used the Fifth Quarto (1613) as copy.[1] The sole authority for the text is the excellent Quarto of 1598. The Quartos do not divide the play into Acts and Scenes. This division is made in the Folios, but with some confusion in Act V.

For the dates of composition we may fix upon 1597 for *Part I* and 1598 for *Part II* without risk of serious error. Francis Meres, writing before October 19, 1598, mentions "Henry the 4" as one of Shakespeare's excellent tragedies (*Palladis Tamia: Wits Treasury,* 1598). Perhaps he means to include both Parts under that title, but his evidence is ambiguous.

For historical materials in both *1 and 2 Henry IV,* as in *Richard II,* Shakespeare went to the second edition of Holinshed's *Chronicles* (1587). The events in *Part I* all come within the limits of almost exactly a year. Sir Edmund Mortimer (whom Shakespeare, like Holinshed, confuses with the Earl of March) was taken prisoner by Glendower on June 22, 1402; the defeat of the Scots at Homildon followed on September 14; on July 21, 1403, Hotspur was killed in the Battle of Shrewsbury— no one knows by whom; Worcester and Vernon were executed two days later. In the play the historical year is reduced to some three or four months.

1 and 2 Henry IV are not the two halves of a single play. Each Part is a drama complete in itself. The word "Part" signifies an historical period—a portion of King Henry's reign—not the division of a dramatic unit. *Part I* and *Part II* are neither tragedies nor comedies. Each of them is a History. This distinction was so well

---

1   Folios were large, expensive books. The First Folio, the first complete edition of Shakespeare's plays produced by two of his fellow actors at the Globe, was printed in 1623. Quartos were cheaply bound single editions of his plays. Often there are key variations between Quarto and Folio texts and modern editors have to decide which version (or a conflation of versions) to present to their readers. There were more Quartos of *1HIV* printed in Shakespeare's lifetime than any other of his plays. See editor's note at conclusiong of Introduction.

understood in Shakespeare's time that it is recognized in the title page of the First Folio: "Mr. William Shakespeares Comedies, Histories, & Tragedies."

The aim of a History (as the term implies) was to bring upon the stage, with a reasonable degree of accuracy, the main events of some period, and to present in action the characters concerned—in their habits as they lived. The requirement of accuracy, however, was not rigorous. It demanded merely that the playwright should not so flagrantly depart from the record as to shock the auditors or to challenge them to contradiction; and there was one department of his task in which he enjoyed liberty that almost amounted to license: namely, in the comic scenes. For such freedom he was indebted to that old-fashioned institution, the Dignity of History, which leaves low life unrecorded, except for an occasional anecdote.

In early plays of this class the comic scenes are often mere interludes that have little or nothing to do with the serious plot. They bring in the stock fun-makers of the stage—the clown or country bumpkin, the ludicrous drunkard, the pickpurse, the braggart or *Miles Gloriosus*, the gull or dupe. In *I Henry IV* we observe a notable contribution to artistic structure: Shakespeare has made the comic scenes an integral part of the drama. And in the present case he enjoyed a matchless opportunity; for the wild youth of Prince Hal was an established tradition: and so, in his character, we have the connecting link between the serious matter and the merry-making. His riots are a vital element in the King's tragedy. Further, by a felicitous device that is all his own, Shakespeare has unified the whole by so developing the character of Hotspur as to bring him into sharp contrast with the Prince, not only in fact but also in the mind of the grief-stricken father (1. 1. 70–90). For bringing Prince Hal and Hotspur into rivalry as youthful aspirants for martial honor Shakespeare had no warrant in history. The Battle of Shrewsbury was fought when the Prince was only sixteen years old. It was his first military experience and he gave proof of that valor for which he was afterwards so famous. Harry Percy was then some forty years of age and had won his pennon in 1378 at the siege of Berwick, a quarter of a century earlier.[2] In the play, the Prince rescues his father at Shrewsbury and kills Hotspur in hand-to-hand combat. These exploits bring the play to a happy ending and establish young Henry's position as the future hero-king. For neither of them had Shakespeare any historical authority. Who rescued the King is not recorded. We know that Percy fell in the battle, but we do not know who killed him, nor does history record any personal encounter between him and the Prince.

The connection between *Richard II* and *1 Henry IV* is close. Bolingbroke's character, well intimated in *Richard II*, is so developed in the later play that he becomes, as King Henry, one of the most baffling of all Shakespeare's complex creatures. He is genuinely patriotic. He had the good of his country at heart, and not merely personal advantage, when he deposed King Richard. His anxiety about his dissolute son is not paternal only: it is largely due to his fear of what will happen

---

2   A *pennon* is a distinctive flag (a symbol of military achievement) attached to the lance of a knight. Henry IV was born in 1367; Prince Henry in 1387. Hotspur was a little older than the King. He was born in 1364.

to England if another Harry shows himself another Richard in instability and tyrannical license. And so, profound dissembler though he is, he actually lays bare his own dissimulation in admonishing his son:

> And then I stole all courtesy from heaven,
> And dress'd myself in such humility
> That I did pluck allegiance from men's hearts,
> Loud shouts and salutations from their mouths
> Even in the presence of the crowned King. (3.2.50ff.)

This whole speech would be almost cynical, were it not for the passionate intensity which submerges the cynicism of its outspokenness.

Prince Hal does not appear in *Richard II*, but his riotous conduct and his companionship with highwaymen are deplored by his father in 5. 3 where Hotspur's scorn of him, so hotly uttered in *1 Henry IV* (1. 3. 230 ff.), comes out by implication in his answer to King Henry's question. Before he began *Part I*, Shakespeare had somewhat modified his former conception of the Prince's character. In *Richard II* he is called "as dissolute as desperate." In *1 Henry IV*, on the contrary, he is neither desperate nor, in the full sense of the word, dissolute. His riots are mere frolics. He does not get drunk and is never involved in any scandal with a woman. Shakespeare, indeed, is so much concerned to guard against misconception on the part of the audience, that he deliberately renounces dramatic propriety in the famous soliloquy at the end of 1.2. This is, in effect, the author's explanation—a kind of chorus—and should be so understood. It is not the expression of the Prince's actual motive in upholding "the unyoked humor" of his riotous comrades. It amounts to a mere statement of fact made by Shakespeare himself: "When the Prince turns over a new leaf, he will be all the more admired for the contrast."[3]

When Shakespeare wrote *1 Henry IV* he gave to the character whom we know as Falstaff the name of Sir John Oldcastle, which he took from *The Famous Victories of Henry the Fifth*. This he changed to Falstaff before the play was printed. Traces of the change appear in the text of both parts. In PART I, the Prince calls him "my old lad of the castle" (1. 2. 47); and one line (2. 2. 115), though not unmetrical as it stands, would be more regular if "Oldcastle" were read instead of "Falstaff." In *Part II*, a speech of Falstaff's (1. 2. 137) is still marked *Old.* in the Quarto of 1600; the Epilogue expressly declares that "Oldcastle died a martyr, and this is not the man." The historical Sir John Oldcastle (called Lord Cobham in his wife's right) was executed for heresy in 1417. The Cobham family was powerful in Shakespeare's time and no doubt protested against the profanation of what to them was a sacred name. For a substitute, Shakespeare went back to *1 Henry VI*, in which one Sir John Fastolfe plays a coward's part, and borrowed the name, with a shift of letters. Perhaps this choice suggested itself because the Prince accuses Oldcastle-Falstaff of

---

3   This is a complex and complicated moment in the play and Kittredge's interpretation of Hal's soliloquy should be regarded as one of many plausible explanations for his behavior rather than being considered definitive.

cowardice in 2.4, after the robbers have been robbed; but Falstaff is not a coward in fact, though traditional interpretation has heedlessly taken the Prince's practical joke as if it justified the accusation.

To analyze a joke may be tedious, but, in the present instance, some scanning of details appears to be obligatory. Falstaff and his three companions, having robbed the travellers, are off their guard and engaged in dividing the spoil when they are stampeded by a surprise attack. They think the officers are upon them in full force. Bardolph and Gadshill and Peto decamp without striking a blow. Falstaff, thus deserted, fences a bit with his two assailants and then runs away also. Why not? He is not a soldier on guard, bound, if need be, to sacrifice his life for his country. He is a highwayman in danger of arrest—and the penalty for robbery was hanging. The point of the jest lies, not in Falstaff's taking to his heels, but in his upbraiding the Prince and Poins for cowardice and thus enabling them to turn the tables; for it was he who ran—not they.

The test of Falstaff's courage comes at the Battle of Shrewsbury, where, if he is a coward, he certainly has the worst luck that ever dogged the steps of a poltroon. He commanded a company of a hundred and fifty foot soldiers, and he led them into the thick of the fight, where they were practically annihilated. Wherever we find him in the field, there we find also the Prince or the doughty Douglas or the heroic Percy. When he soliloquized upon honor, he repudiated it as "a mere scutcheon" and declared that he had no desire for it; but when the time comes for action, he is always where he ought to be—in the center of the field. To be sure, he saves his life by a stratagem when there is nothing to be gained by sacrificing it. But, again, why not? He knows the difference between valor and foolhardiness. He is a veteran officer who has had fighting enough in the past and does not love danger for its own sake. After all, Douglas also tries to escape and Hal regards him as a man of military honor deserving of pardon.

George Lyman Kittredge

Editor's Note

I have retained all of Kittredge's introduction except for some historical material and literary references that seemed dated. I have also trimmed, but not eliminated, his repeated attempts to defend Falstaff from potential detractors. All of the explanatory footnotes are mine.

Samuel Crowl

INTRODUCTION TO THE FOCUS EDITION

I HENRY IV is Shakespeare at his most dazzling: epic in scope, festive in spirit, ironic in structure. The play is the second in a quartet of interrelated historical dramas dealing with events in English history between the usurpation and murder of Richard II in 1399 and the marriage of Henry V to Princess Katherine of France in 1420. But moving from Shakespeare's *Richard II* to his *1 Henry IV* is like moving from one world to another; moving from the ornate, hierarchical patterns of the melodramatic and medieval into the fluid, shape-shifting, political and psychological realities of the modern.

Shakespeare's achievement in the history play genre reached its zenith in *1 Henry IV*. The play is epic in its reach because the fate of England hangs in the balance as Henry IV attempts to consolidate his reign and successfully pass the crown on to his son; it is festive in spirit because Falstaff presides over the tavern world like the Lord of Misrule at Carnival; and it is ironic in structure because the various plot strands of the play repeatedly challenge and comment upon one another "minding true things by what their mock'ries be."(*HV.* 4.1.53)

In *1 Henry IV* Shakespeare produces a work that bristles with energy and ideas. He returns to the use of multiple plots or narrative strands that had served him so well in *A Midsummer Night's Dream*. Now he infuses them with an artistically shrewd grasp of the ways in which the public and the personal can be made to comment upon each other as the political fissure in the country provoked by the Percy's rebellion is mirrored in the king's alienation from his son and heir. After his father's overthrow of Richard II, the master narrative of the four play sequence becomes Prince Hal's reformation and rise to power culminating in his victory over France at the Battle of Agincourt in *Henry V*. In *1 Henry IV* Shakespeare dramatically divides that narrative into three plot strands: the king's attempt to unite the country under his leadership and successfully pass the crown on to a worthy dynastic heir; Hotspur's rebellion which seeks to wrench the crown from Henry's hands in the name of honor and feudal chivalry; and Falstaff's subversive intent to transform every day into holiday. Prince Hal is the character who unites these narrative strands. He is central to each and is the only character in the play that moves successfully between his father's court, Falstaff's tavern, and Hotspur's battlefield.

The first two acts quickly establish the three major landscapes of the play: court, tavern, and rebel camp. The king presides over a court and country in crisis as his rule and legitimacy are challenged by the very same nobles who initially supported him in his move against Richard II and by the wayward behavior of his son. Falstaff presides over the tavern where care and responsibility are banished in the name of high-spirited play; Hotspur presides over the rebel world with the flash of his fiery energy, admirable in battle but a liability in coalition-building among his rebel partners. After the two tavern scenes featuring Falstaff and Hal (2.4 and 3.3) the three plot strands, having developed on parallel lines, begin to move to their intersection at the Battle of Shrewsbury, where for the first time all four major figures will occupy the same landscape.

When reading the play it is easy to hold these powerful personalities in balance and to see that Hal's sharp political cunning assesses how each (king, rival, surrogate father) can aid him in the reformation of his image, the reclamation of his father's confidence, and the realization of his rise to power. In performance, however, Falstaff and Hotspur (and in some productions I have seen, even the king) tend to dominate and eclipse Hal's centrality. Falstaff's wit and infinite energy command our attention in his scenes with the Prince even as we may see, as he surely does not, the cold threat that lies behind Hal's promise (when playing his father) eventually to banish him: "I do. I will." (2.4.463) Hotspur is equally vivid and vigorous and even surprisingly witty (Glendower [exasperated]: "I can call spirits from the vasty deep." Hotspur [cocky]: "Why, so can I, or so can any man,/But do they come when you do call for them?"(3.1.50-52) Falstaff makes us laugh **and** think: a powerful and winning combination. Hotspur appeals to our love for the rebel unsullied by political calculation (that element of the rebellion is left to his uncle Worcester to embody). The king, though hoping to lead a pilgrimage to the Holy Lands to unite England under one banner and to assuage his guilt for the overthrow and murder of Richard II, is seriously concerned for the fate of his country and expresses the genuine if misguided fear of the CEO that his playboy son is not quite up to the job of succeeding him.

On stage it is hard to hold Hal in steady focus against this trio of heady rivals for our attention. He is a subtle shape-shifter who has learned well the art of role-playing from his master teacher, Falstaff. The key to Hal's character is his brilliant command of language. In the first great tavern scene, he boasts: "I can drink with any tinker in his own language." (2.4.15-16). Hal can banter with tinkers and tapsters, trade barbs and quote scripture with Falstaff, and reassure the king in the language of political commerce that executive fathers best understand: "Percy is but my factor, good my lord,/To engross up glorious deeds on my behalf,/And I will call him to so strict account/That he shall render every glory up,/Yea, even the slightest worship of his time,/Or I will tear the reckoning from his heart." (3.2. 146-152) The prince's use of "factor," "account," "engross," and "reckoning" redefines the chivalric clash between Hal and Hotspur into the pragmatic "business" of politics. And when the two dashing young men finally do confront one another, it turns out that Hal can speak the language of steel as well, as he beats Hotspur at his own game and on his own turf.

Shakespeare also uses language to enrich the resonances between the high and low, heroic and mock-heroic, conventional and radical plot levels. Hotspur dismisses Hal as "the mad-cap Prince of Wales" who could be "poisoned with a pot of ale"; while Hal mocks his rival as that "Hotspur of the north, he that kills me six or seven dozen Scots at a breakfast, washes his hands, and says to his wife, 'Fie upon this quiet life, I want work.'" (2.4.89-91) Hal wants to "redeem" time while Hotspur wants to "redeem" honor, and that captures the crucial difference between the two rivals for power. Hal has the modern politician's sense of image and timing, while Hotspur covets action over strategy. Hotspur thinks it would be "an easy leap to pluck bright honor from the pale-faced moon," (1.3.201-202) while Falstaff interrogates honor and finds it just a "word. What is in that word honor? ... Air. ... Who hath it? He that died a' Wednesday." (5.1.136) The king "counterfeits" by having many men marching in his "coats" while Falstaff "counterfeits" by pretending to be dead as the battle of Shrewsbury swirls about him. Falstaff's apparent cowardice makes us revise our judgment both about his behavior and the king's military strategy. Hal steals purses from Falstaff at Gad's Hill and Falstaff pays him back by stealing a Percy at Shrewsbury.

Shakespeare makes the linguistic echoes and puns insistent and irresistible. The play ends with the heroic and mock-heroic still held in tension without the triumph of one mode over the other. Hal has defeated Hotspur and handsomely sung his praises in an epitaph to the chivalric tradition he represents. He then stumbles over Falstaff's fallen body, and dismisses his expansive friend with three tidy rhyming couplets thinking he has escaped Falstaff's shadow as well as Hotspur's. But the mock heroic—unlike Hotspur, who plays for keeps—just won't die. Falstaff arises from the dead, gives Hotspur a new wound in the thigh (the comedy verging on sacrilege here), and carts his prize off to one-up Hal for the final time in the play. Hal has managed to vanquish one of the threats to his reformation but not the other, and Shakespeare is free to extend the Hal-Falstaff relationship into *2 Henry IV* , where it is coldly resolved.

For audiences and critics, Falstaff dominates the play. He is one of Shakespeare's most unique creations who is an amalgam of many established stereotypes from the ancient Braggart Soldier of Roman Comedy and the Vice figure from the Medieval Morality Play to the giant "Power Baby" and excluded "other" of postmodern theory. But most significantly he is the Lord of Misrule who presides over Carnival. The tavern, of course, is his natural setting, but Shakespeare brazenly takes him on the road to Shrewsbury where he bumps into and directly comments upon the hard political and military realities of the play. The epic confrontation with the rebels is as crucial to the king's legacy as the clash with Hotspur is to Hal's reformation, but Falstaff understands that many of the nameless will die in this encounter though they have little stake in its outcome. When Hal chastises Falstaff for the "pitiful rascals" he has recruited to fight, Falstaff reminds him (and us) of the blunt truth: "Tut, tut, good enough to toss, food for powder, food for powder, they'll fill a pit as well as better. Tush, man, mortal men, mortal men." (4.3. 54-56). Shakespeare daringly stretches comedy and misrule to its limits here and again at the end of the play when he has the clown claim the fallen hero as his prize as he waddles off the stage and into the world of myth.

Performance History

1 Henry IV was an immediate hit when it was first produced in late 1596 or early 1597. The quick surfacing of the Oldcastle issue (see Kittredge's introduction, p. ix, for details) shows that the play struck a pronounced chord with its audience and led to the immediate publication of two quarto (single volume) editions of the play in 1598. They were followed by five more such editions in 1599, 1604, 1608, 1613 and 1622, making *1 Henry IV* the most oft-printed Shakespeare play script in its time. Shakespeare probably wrote the part of Falstaff for the first great clown in his company, Will Kemp. We do not know, however, if his leading man, Richard Burbage, played Hal or Hotspur. The actor-managers who dominated the English theater in the 17th, 18th, and 19th centuries, starting with Thomas Betterton, were much more likely to perform either Hotspur or Falstaff than Hal. In fact, Betterton performed both, beginning with Hotspur in 1682 and moving on to play Falstaff for many seasons beginning in 1700. The tradition of the actors playing Hotspur and Falstaff overshadowing those who played Hal and the king continued from the 18th to the mid-20th century culminating in a production at the Old Vic theater in 1945 starring Ralph Richardson as Falstaff and Laurence Olivier as Hotspur. Richardson's Falstaff was considered his greatest Shakespearean performance and has lingered in the memories of many 20th century Shakespeare critics, most notably Harold Bloom. Olivier gave his Hotspur a stammer on words beginning with the letter "w", adding to the pathos of the character's death as he tried and failed to say "worms", thus dying on a final stammer. Accounts of the production rarely mention the actor, Michael Warre, who played Hal. His stage career, like those of many Hals before him, was undistinguished.

That tradition was soon to change with the next major production of the play in England. With the development of a repertory company at Stratford-upon-Avon after World War II, culminating in the creation of the Royal Shakespeare Company in 1960, came an interest in performing seasons of what has come to be known as "epic Shakespeare." The first, to celebrate the Festival of Britain in 1951, was Stratford's mounting of unified productions of *1* and *2 Henry IV* and *Henry V* under the direction of Anthony Quayle. Quayle played Falstaff but he cast the brilliant young Welsh actor, Richard Burton, as Hal. As it became increasingly popular to stage the three plays (and sometimes even *Richard II* as well) together, the part of Hal became more attractive to actors. Subsequent Hals in major multiple play productions in England have included Ian Holm (1960), Alan Howard (1975), Gerard Murphy (1982), Michael Maloney (1991), Michael Houston (2000), and Geoffrey Streatfeild (2007) for the Royal Shakespeare Company; Michael Pennington (1985-87) for the English Shakespeare Company; and Michael Macfadyan (2005) for the National Theater. The Falstaffs in some of these productions remained strong with John Woodvine (1985), Robert Stephens, (1991), Desmond Barrit (2000), Michael Gambon (2005), and David Warner (2007) winning prizes and plaudits for their performances. As Hal's star rose in performance, Hotspur's plummeted. The only Hotspur in the six productions mentioned above who made a vivid impression was

Andrew Jarvis for the English Shakespeare Company and he was the third actor to play the role in the long three year run of the company's production of the complete cycle of Shakespeare's history plays from *Richard II* to *Richard III*, mounted under the title: *The Wars of the Roses*.

In North America, the Stratford Shakespeare Festival of Canada has produced several productions of the play, the best being the first (1958) with Douglas Campbell as a robustly comic Falstaff and Jason Robards, Jr. as a memorable Hotspur. The most recent production in New York at Lincoln Center (2003), a one play compilation of *Henry IV, Parts One and Two*, reverted to the tradition where the Falstaff (Kevin Kline) and Hotspur (Ethan Hawke) overshadowed Hal (Michael Hayden) and his father (Richard Easton). Kline was a fine Falstaff who found the humor in Falstaff's words and let them do the work rather than plumping up his performance with lots of comic stage business. Kline was a congenial Falstaff rather than a seedy opportunist, but he also made us realize that Falstaff's intelligence was far too keen and subversive to survive in the world of Henry V. An earlier production of this version of the two plays had been performed at San Diego's Old Globe Theater in 1995 with the film and television star John Goodman finding Falstaff a perfect fit for his comic abilities.

The Play on Film and Television

1 Henry IV exists in two wonderfully divergent television productions from the British Broadcasting Company (BBC) and the English Shakespeare Company (ESC) and a brilliant movie, *Chimes at Midnight* (1966), directed by Orson Welles. All three productions are available on video and DVD. Welles's movie, considered one of the finest Shakespeare films ever made, creates a single two hour narrative of the Hal-Falstaff story, based on material derived primarily from *Henry IV, Parts One and Two*.

Chimes at Midnight actually contains more material from *1 Henry IV* but draws its atmosphere and emphasis from *2 Henry IV*. As the title suggests, the film concentrates on Falstaff and begins with Falstaff (Welles) and Shallow (a character from *2 Henry IV* here played by Alan Webb) working their way slowly through a wintry landscape and into a great wood-beamed hall to settle before a roaring fire as Shallow cackles: "Jesu, Sir John, the days that we have seen." To which Falstaff rumbles his famous reply: "We have heard the chimes at midnight, Master Shallow." This brief prologue establishes the film as a flashback with Falstaff at the center of its focus. Falstaff's preeminence is further underlined by the film's final shot which captures Bardolph and Peto and Poins pushing a cart, holding his giant coffin, out through the inn yard of the Boar's Head Tavern on its way to the grave.

Welles, in direction and performance, makes no secret of his affection for Falstaff. He knows Falstaff is a rogue but he plays him as a warm and generous one, particularly in his involvement with Hal. The two men exhibit a playful, tactile relationship with one another and the film nicely captures the energy released in their interaction. Welles is fond of shooting Falstaff from a low angle perspective, often framed against the wooden beams of the tavern or the open sky, thus enlarging his image in the frame and associating him with the warmth of the wood or the expanse of the sky. The king (John Gielgud), in contrast, is most often captured standing alone on a high platform and shot against the cold stone of the film's setting for the Westminster scenes, emphasizing his isolation from his family and court community and the potential impasse of his political predicament. Keith Baxter's Hal is appropriately impish and fun-loving in his early encounters with Falstaff but we can see his eyes narrow and his jaw tighten when he delivers the line: "I do. I will," forecasting his eventual rejection of his old companion. That same look has hardened into his everyday face by the time he has been crowned and confronts Falstaff who has rushed to interrupt his coronation procession with his fatherly desire to embrace "My sweet boy. My king...my Jove." (text lifted and slightly rearranged from *2 Henry IV*).

Hotspur's character suffers the most in Welles's trimming of the text; he emerges less as a free and fiery spirit and more as just a simple foil to Hal's reformation. Welles's treatment of the battle of Shrewsbury is justly famous as one of film's great battle scenes. The battle is not an epic clash but a brutal destructive rite conducted by mud-laden soldiers in which the two sides become indistinguishable from one another. Hotspur and Hal's duel mirrors the larger battle by reducing the two valiant heroes to exhausted boxers simply trying to survive the 15th round of a championship fight. The winner becomes the man who has the energy and strength to lift his sword for one final blow. Welles's *Chimes at Midnight* demonstrates what the bold and imaginative director can accomplish when adapting Shakespeare for film. Here Shakespeare is translated into image and action that manages to capture the spirit of his text without a slavish devotion to it and in the process a new work is created: a genuine film based upon but not fatally tethered to its source.

The BBC television production of *1 Henry IV* (1979) presents us with a traditional, some would say conservative, approach to the play. Following the general guidelines for the series, the BBC production is set in the play's historical period with Henry IV (Jon Finch) costumed to resemble surviving portraits of the king. The director, David Giles, shoots much of the dialogue in medium close-up realizing that television is not a medium which can give us the epic reach of the play. This decision works well for the Hal (David Gwillim) and Falstaff (Anthony Quayle) exchanges where the flash of witty word-play is at a premium. It works less well for Tim Pigott-Smith's Hotspur who needs the expanse of a more cinematic landscape to capture his rebel posture and impassioned rhetoric. Gwillim's Hal is distinguished by his carefree attitude (the actor has an attractive mouth that can be stretched into a wide smile) and reveals little of the cool manipulator some actors find in the character. Quayle's Falstaff is a bit too eager to please his royal companion and seems always to be anxiously waiting to see how his witticisms have been received rather than self-confidently riding the wave of his comic intelligence. Finch's Henry IV is defined by a series of nervous hand gestures that seem to signal his guilt for the overthrow of Richard II but may also be motivated by the historical suggestion (not present in Shakespeare's play) that the king suffered from a venereal disease.

The ESC version of the play takes all the chances the BBC production studiously avoids. The production was conceived for the stage and began as part of a three play cycle (*Henry IV, Parts One and Two* and *Henry V*) that grew over a period of several years to a seven play cycle encompassing Shakespeare's major English history plays. The cycle toured England, several European countries, Japan, Canada and America. The seven plays were recorded for television before a live audience in Swansea, Wales on the last weekend of their run. The play's director, Michael Bogdanov, champions the idea that Shakespeare is our contemporary and repeatedly costumes his Shakespeare productions in modern dress. In his production of *1 Henry IV* the costuming is 20th century eclectic with the king dressed in a black frock coat and striped trousers of the early 20th century while Hal and the Boar's Head tavern crowd are dressed in jeans and leather mini-skirts and punk paraphernalia with Gadshill sporting a Mohawk haircut. Some of the tavern crew wear leather jackets with Hal's Angels embroidered on the back. The tavern scenes are staged with lots of music, dancing, and physical energy in contrast to the static and somber atmosphere of Henry IV's court.

Barry Stanton's Falstaff is conceived as a slightly down-on-his-heels aristocrat with a mischievous twinkle in his eye but certainly poses no threat, directly or indirectly, to the state. Michael Pennington's Hal, a bit older than we might imagine the character, is nevertheless not as fully formed or in command of his persona from the beginning, as his soliloquy in 1.2 might suggest. Pennington is clearly emotionally upset when his interview with his father in 3.2 does not end in the gesture of reconciliation the text might warrant. Frustrated, Pennington slams his foot up against his father's desk after the king has exited with Sir Walter Blunt. Pennington replays this emotional ambiguity in the final confrontation with Hotspur. He loses his sword in the fight and cowers in fear, waiting for Hotspur to strike the fatal blow, but his rival refuses to dispatch an unarmed opponent so he slides his sword back to him. The duel recommences until Hal wounds Hotspur and again seems emotionally paralyzed before striking the final, fatal blow. The production was intended, much like Baz Luhrmann's film of *William Shakespeare's Romeo + Juliet*, to appeal to a younger audience with little previous knowledge of Shakespeare or experience of seeing his plays in performance. The production itself wanted to shake up more experienced Shakespeare-goers much as Falstaff's blunt humor means to shake up the establishment in the world of the play.

Adaptations

One of the key narratives in *1 Henry IV* is archetypal: the tension and conflict between the powerful father and the wayward son. Shakespeare refines the archetype by including a surrogate father-figure who temporarily complicates the young man's development into his own secure identity. Such coming-of-age stories are ubiquitous in modern fiction and film and all might be said to owe some debt to Shakespeare's working of this territory in both *1 Henry IV* and *Hamlet*. The only contemporary film which draws directly and openly on parallels both with Shakespeare's history play and with Orson Welles's *Chimes at Midnight* is Gus Van Sant's *My Own Private Idaho*. Van Sant's film presents an intertwined double plot which follows the fates of two young men, Scott and Mike. The two are street hustlers in Portland, Oregon. They come from very different class backgrounds but both come from incomplete and dysfunctional families. Scott is the Hal figure. His father is the mayor of Portland and Scott knows that some day he will have to accept the responsibility of being his politically powerful father's son. Scott has become friends with the seedy leader of Portland street life, Bob Pigeon. Bob is the Falstaff figure and many of his scenes with Scott not only have direct parallels to scenes in Shakespeare's play but are shot in homage to Welles's camera work in *Chimes at Midnight*. The film is the most radical and cinematically daring of the Shakespeare adaptations that have emerged in the last two decades, including *10 Things I Hate About You*, *O*, and *Scotland, PA*.

Samuel Crowl
2009

Editor's Note

The only major changes I have made to Kittredge's excellent notes are to excise his obvious relish in cross-referencing both other works of the period as well as Shakespeare's other plays. I do not believe that the modern reader interested in Shakespeare in performance will find this material helpful in confronting the text. I have retained his few cross-references to Biblical passages, and added a few of my own, because they constitute a lively source of the wit that flows between Falstaff and Hal. Kittredge's evident need to defend Falstaff (who surely is his own finest apologist) finds its way into the notes where I tried, as I did in his Introduction, to trim rather than eliminate his remarks. I have annotated several words, phrases, or references that Kittredge probably found self-explanatory but, with the passage of time, have slipped out of common usage. I have indicated all such efforts by [s.c.] to distinguish them from Kittredge's work.

THE FIRST PART OF KING HENRY THE FOURTH

DRAMATIS PERSONAE

King Henry the Fourth.
Henry, Prince of Wales, ⎱ sons of the *King.*
Prince John of Lancaster, ⎰
Earl of Westmoreland.
Sir Walter Blunt.
Thomas Percy, Earl of Worcester.
Henry Percy, Earl of Northumberland.
Henry Percy, surnamed *Hotspur,* his son.
Edmund Mortimer, Earl of March.
Richard Scroop, Archbishop of York.
Archibald, Earl of Douglas.
Owen Glendower.
Sir Richard Vernon.
Sir John Falstaff.
Sir Michael, a friend to the *Archbishop of York.*
Poins.
Gadshill.
Peto.
Bardolph.

Lady Percy, wife to *Hotspur,* and sister to *Mortimer.*
Lady Mortimer, daughter to *Glendower,* and wife to *Mortimer.*
Mistress Quickly, hostess of the Boar's Head in Eastcheap.

Lords, Officers, Sheriff, Vintner, Chamberlain, Drawers, two Carriers, Travellers, and Attendants.

SCENE.—*England and Wales*

1

ACT I

SCENE I. [*London. The Palace.*]

Enter the King, Lord John of Lancaster, Earl of Westmoreland,
[Sir Walter Blunt,] *with others.*

KING.   So shaken as we are, so wan with care,†
Find we a time for frighted peace to pant
And breathe short-winded accents of new broils
To be commenc'd in stronds afar remote.
No more the thirsty entrance of this soil   5
Shall daub her lips with her own children's blood.
No more shall trenching war channel her fields,
Nor bruise her flow'rets with the armed hoofs
Of hostile paces. Those opposed eyes
Which, like the meteors of a troubled heaven,   10
All of one nature, of one substance bred,
Did lately meet in the intestine shock
And furious close of civil butchery,
Shall now in mutual well-beseeming ranks
March all one way and be no more oppos'd   15
Against acquaintance, kindred, and allies.
The edge of war, like an ill-sheathed knife,
No more shall cut his master. Therefore, friends,
As far as to the sepulchre of Christ—

ACT I. SCENE I.
The scene is set at the king's court, probably at Westminster, in London. King Henry, thinking that the civil war is finished, has called a council to consider the Crusade—the holy war that, in expiation for the death of King Richard, he has vowed to undertake. 2–4. **Find we...remote:** Let us give frighted Peace a chance to breathe, though she must gasp for breath, and to speak pantingly of new wars to be undertaken on far-distant shores (in the Holy Land).—**stronds:** strands, regions. 5, 6. **No more...blood:** No longer shall our native land drink the blood of her own children, staining her lips therewith as she lets it enter (soak into) the soil. 8, 9. **with...of hostile paces:** with the tread of the steeds of troops at war with each other. 10, 11. **like the meteors...bred.** The substance of a meteor was thought to be a gas given out (exhaled) by the sky or by some heavenly body. 13. **close:** hand-to-hand combat. 14. **mutual:** united in a common purpose. 19. **As far as:** for an expedition whose object is as far distant as.

---

†   To suggest the public nature of the king's opening speech, the English Shakespeare Company's (ESC) stage production of the play (set in a period that ranged from roughly 1915-1965) had Henry IV delivering his remarks into a radio microphone as though he were addressing the nation. This device had been eliminated three years later when the play was taped for television. In Welles's film, the speech is regarded as a more private statement of the king's troubled conscience. The king's care and concern is magnified by having Henry's throne situated on an elevated platform with the king (John Gielgud) repeatedly shot from a low angle perspective further emphasizing his isolation. [s.c.]

	Whose soldier now, under whose blessed cross	20
	We are impressed and engag'd to fight—	

Whose soldier now, under whose blessed cross   20
We are impressed and engag'd to fight—
Forthwith a power of English shall we levy,
Whose arms were moulded in their mother's womb
To chase these pagans in those holy fields
Over whose acres walk'd those blessed feet   25
Which fourteen hundred years ago were nail'd
For our advantage on the bitter cross.
But this our purpose now is twelvemonth old,
And bootless 'tis to tell you we will go.
Therefore we meet not now. Then let me hear   30
Of you, my gentle cousin Westmoreland,
What yesternight our Council did decree
In forwarding this dear expedience.

WEST.   My liege, this haste was hot in question
And many limits of the charge set down   35
But yesternight; when all athwart there came
A post from Wales, loaden with heavy news;
Whose worst was that the noble Mortimer,
Leading the men of Herefordshire to fight
Against the irregular and wild Glendower,   40
Was by the rude hands of that Welshman taken,
A thousand of his people butchered;
Upon whose dead corpse there was such misuse,
Such beastly shameless transformation,
By those Welshwomen done as may not be   45
Without much shame retold or spoken of.

KING.   It seems then that the tidings of this broil
Brake off our business for the Holy Land.

---

21. **We.** The royal *we*: "I, the King."—**impressed.** The King speaks of himself as if he were a conscript, enlisted by compulsion. His *vow* is the conscripting authority.—**engag'd:** pledged. 22. **a power:** an army. 29. **bootless:** useless.—**go. Therefore.** Both words are emphatic: "There is no point in my telling you that it is my purpose to go; not for *that* reason is this meeting called, but to consider the necessary preparations." 31. **gentle:** noble.—**cousin.** The Earl was related to King Henry by marriage, but not his cousin in the limited modern sense. *Cousin* is used to indicate almost any relationship except that of direct descent. 32. **decree:** decide. 33–35. **this dear expedience:** the urgent promptitude of this important expedition. *This haste* repeats the idea.—**hot in question:** earnestly debated.—**limits of the charge:** estimates of the necessary cost. 36, 37. **all athwart:** quite across the path—i.e., so as to interrupt the course of our deliberations by unfavourable news.—**A post:** a messenger riding posthaste. 38. **Mortimer.** Shakespeare, following Holinshed, represents this to be Edmund Mortimer, Earl of March. In fact, it was the Earl's uncle, Sir Edmund Mortimer, who was captured by Glendower on June 22, 1402, and who married Glendower's daughter. Lady Percy was Sir Edmund's sister. 40. **irregular.** This adjective describes Glendower as engaged in "guerrilla" warfare, as contrasted with a "regular" army. 43. **corpse:** corpses.—**misuse:** abuse, castration [s.c.] 44, 45. **transformation.** A mild word for "mutilation." Cf. Holinshed: "The shamefull villanie vsed by the Welshwomen towards the dead carcasses, was such as honest eares would be ashamed to heare, and continent toongs to speake thereof."—**may:** can.

King Henry IV (John Gielgud) framed against the cold stone walls of the Westminster Palace. (Welles's *Chimes at Midnight*)

WEST.	This, match'd with other, did, my gracious lord;	
	For more uneven and unwelcome news	50
	Came from the North, and thus it did import:	
	On Holy-rood Day the gallant Hotspur there,	
	Young Harry Percy, and brave Archibald,	
	That ever-valiant and approved Scot,	
	At Holmedon met,	55
	Where they did spend a sad and bloody hour;	
	As by discharge of their artillery	
	And shape of likelihood the news was told;	
	For he that brought them, in the very heat	
	And pride of their contention did take horse,	60
	Uncertain of the issue any way.	
KING.	Here is a dear, a true-industrious friend,	
	Sir Walter Blunt, new lighted from his horse,	
	Stain'd with the variation of each soil	
	Betwixt that Holmedon and this seat of ours,	65
	And he hath brought us smooth and welcome news.	

50, 51. **uneven:** rough, disconcerting.—**import:** signify. 52. **Holy-rood Day:** September the fourteenth, the day consecrated to the Holy Cross. The year was 1402. 53. **brave:** noble.—**Archibald:** Earl of Douglas. 54, 55. **approved:** of well-tested valor.—**Holmedon:** In Northumberland. 58. **shape of likelihood:** probable inference. 60. **pride.** Synonymous with *heat*: "intensity." 62. **true-industrious:** sincerely devoted. 66. **smooth:** pleasant. Antithetic to *uneven* in l. 50.

King Henry IV (Jon Finch) rubbing his gloved and guilty hands. (BBC-TVs *1 Henry IV*)

The Earl of Douglas is discomfited;
Ten thousand bold Scots, two-and-twenty knights,
Balk'd in their own blood did Sir Walter see
On Holmedon's plains. Of prisoners, Hotspur took   70
Mordake Earl of Fife and eldest son
To beaten Douglas, and the Earl of Athol,
Of Murray, Angus, and Menteith.
And is not this an honourable spoil?
A gallant prize? Ha, cousin, is it not?   75

WEST.   In faith,
It is a conquest for a prince to boast of.

KING.   Yea, there thou mak'st me sad, and mak'st me sin
In envy that my Lord Northumberland
Should be the father to so blest a son—   80
A son who is the theme of honor's tongue,
Amongst a grove the very straightest plant;
Who is sweet Fortune's minion and her pride;
Whilst I, by looking on the praise of him,

---

69. **Balk'd in their own blood:** piled up in ridges and soaked in blood. A *balk* is the ridge between two furrows. 71. **Mordake.** He was the son of the Duke of Albany. Shakespeare was misled by a misprint in Holinshed. 77. **prince.** Emphatic: "even a prince." 78. **there.** Emphatic: "by using that word *prince.*" 82. **plant:** tree. 83. **minion:** darling, favorite [s.c.]

See riot and dishonor stain the brow   85
Of my young Harry. O that it could be prov'd
That some night-tripping fairy had exchang'd
In cradle clothes our children where they lay,
And call'd mine Percy, his Plantagenet!
Then would I have his Harry, and he mine.   90
But let him from my thoughts. What think you, coz,
Of this young Percy's pride? The prisoners
Which he in this adventure hath surpris'd
To his own use he keeps, and sends me word
I shall have none but Mordake Earl of Fife.   95

WEST.   This is his uncle's teaching, this is Worcester,
Malevolent to you in all aspects,
Which makes him prune himself and bristle up
The crest of youth against your dignity.

KING.   But I have sent for him to answer this;   100
And for this cause awhile we must neglect
Our holy purpose to Jerusalem.
Cousin, on Wednesday next our council we
Will hold at Windsor. So inform the lords;
But come yourself with speed to us again;   105
For more is to be said and to be done
Than out of anger can be uttered.

WEST.   I will, my liege.   *Exeunt.*

85, 86. **riot...Harry.** This prepares us for the next scene. 87. **had exchang'd.** Ugly and deformed infants were often thought to be "changelings"—impish creatures left by the fairies in exchange for the babies they had stolen and carried off to fairyland. **Plantagenet.** A surname of the royal family. 90. **would I have,** etc.: i.e., I should insist on making the exchange. 91. **from:** depart from.—**coz:** cousin, kinsman [s.c.] 92. **pride.** Emphatic. 93. **surpris'd:** captured. 94. **To his own use:** for his own profit—since he could gain much from their ransom. 95. **Mordake.** Steevens notes that Percy could not refuse Mordake to King Henry, since Mordake was of royal blood (nephew of the Scottish king) and therefore could be justly claimed by the King of England, whose vassal Percy was. With regard to the other prisoners, however, there was room for argument. 97. **Malevolent...aspécts.** A metaphor from astrology. The *aspect* of a planet is the way in which it "looks upon" one—either with a favourable or a malignant influence. "Worcester is always, and under all circumstances, hostile to you and your interests." 98, 99. **Which.** The antecedent is *teaching.*—**prune himself.** This is explained by the phrase that follows. The figure comes from falconry. A hawk prunes himself when he prepares for action by arranging his feathers with his beak, pruning away such of them as are loose or broken. 101. **neglect:** disregard; lay aside. The word does not carry the modern sense of *culpable* disregard or omission. 107. **Than out of anger can be uttered:** than can be spoken or carried out by us in the heat of anger. "We must not act upon angry impulse, for this crisis requires calm deliberation." 108. **liege:** liege lord—the sovereign to whom I owe allegiance.

SCENE II. [*London. An apartment of the* Prince's.]

Enter Prince of Wales *and* Sir John Falstaff.

FAL.   Now, Hal, what time of day is it, lad?†

PRINCE.   Thou art so fat-witted with drinking of old sack, and unbuttoning thee
            after supper, and sleeping upon benches after noon, that thou hast
            forgotten to demand that truly which thou wouldest truly know. What
            a devil hast thou to do with the time of the day? Unless hours were
            cups of sack, and minutes capons, and clocks the tongues of bawds,
            and dials the signs of leaping houses, and the blessed sun himself a fair
            hot wench in flame-coloured taffeta, I see no reason why thou shouldst
            be so superfluous to demand the time of the day.   9

FAL.   Indeed you come near me now, Hal; for we that take purses go by
            the moon and the seven stars, and not by Phœbus, he, that wand'ring
            knight so fair. And I prithee, sweet wag, when thou art king, as, God
            save thy Grace—Majesty I should say, for grace thou wilt have none—

PRINCE.   What, none?

FAL.   No, by my troth; not so much as will serve to be prologue to an egg
            and butter.   16

PRINCE.   Well, how then? Come, roundly, roundly.

Understood that Hal is going to leave the tavern world

SCENE II

This scene takes place in London at the Prince's residence—certainly not at the royal palace or at
any tavern. 1–9. **Fat-witted:** thick-witted.[s.c.]—**sack:** The old name for sherry and similar wines.—
demand that truly...know: ask that correctly which thou wouldst really know.—**of the day.** *Day* is
emphatic. Prince Hal regards Falstaff as a night bird.—**taffeta:** a kind of silk.—**so superfluous:** so
given to useless talk.—**to:** as to. 10–13. **you come near me:** you have scored a point on me. Literally,
the phrase means "have just missed hitting me" (in fencing or sword play).—**go by.** A mild pun: (1)
"walk about by the light of"; (2) "count time by"—for the *night* is the only time for us.—**the seven
stars:** the Pleiades.—**wand'ring knight:** knight errant. The Knight of the Sun is the hero of a chivalric
romance popular in Shakespeare's day. See 3.3.20 note.—**sweet.** Very common as a mere synonym for
"dear."—**wag:** rogue, fellow. —**Grace.** *Your grace* and *your Highness* were often used for "your Majesty."
Falstaff's pun is obvious: "You'll not have a bit of virtue or goodness." 15–16. **my troth:** my faith.—**an
egg and butter.** For so slight a meal, Falstaff suggests, a very brief "grace before meat" would suffice. 17.
roundly, roundly: Speak out in plain terms—what is it you wish to ask me to do when I am King?

†   In many productions Falstaff's question is preceded by some horse-play where Hal is waking his
        old companion up after a night of heavy drinking. As a twist on this tradition, in the National
        Theatre's (NT) recent (2005) stage production, Falstaff (Michael Gambon) and Hal (Michael
        Macfadyan) entered and, turning their backs to the audience, drunkenly relieved their bladders
        and amused themselves by seeing who could produce the highest arc in urinating. When Falstaff
        finished he turned to Hal to deliver the first line of the scene. More modestly, in New York's
        Lincoln Center production (2003) Falstaff (Kevin Kline) was slumped down against one of the
        tavern's support timbers. When Hal (Michael Hayden) awoke him, Kline reached out with his
        walking stick; Hal grabbed on to it and helped him to his feet establishing the rise and fall pattern
        of their relationship. [s.c.]

FAL.   Marry, then, sweet wag, when thou art king, let not us that are squires
of the night's body be called thieves of the day's beauty. Let us be
Diana's Foresters, Gentlemen of the Shade, Minions of the Moon;
and let men say we be men of good government, being governed as
the sea is, by our noble and chaste mistress the moon, under whose
countenance we steal.   23

PRINCE. Thou sayest well, and it holds well too; for the fortune of us that are
the moon's men doth ebb and flow like the sea, being governed, as the
sea is, by the moon. As, for proof now: a purse of gold most resolutely
snatch'd on Monday night and most dissolutely spent on Tuesday
morning; got with swearing 'Lay by,' and spent with crying 'Bring in';
now in as low an ebb as the foot of the ladder, and by-and-by in as
high a flow as the ridge of the gallows.   30

FAL.   By the Lord, thou say'st true, lad—and is not my hostess of the tavern
a most sweet wench?   *was going to be call oldcastle - sensorship*

PRINCE. As the honey of Hybla, my old lad of the castle—and is not a buff
jerkin a most sweet robe of durance?

FAL.   How now, how now, mad wag? What, in thy quips and thy quiddities?
What a plague have I to do with a buff jerkin?   36

PRINCE. Why, what a pox have I to do with my hostess of the tavern?

FAL.   Well, thou hast call'd her to a reckoning many a time and oft.

PRINCE. Did I ever call for thee to pay thy part?

---

18. **Marry.** Originally an oath by the Virgin Mary, but used as a mere interjection. 18–23. **squires of the night's body.** A squire of the body was a personal attendant on a knight. The puns are relentless in the Hal-Falstaff exchanges; both have a keen enjoyment of verbal sparring [s.c.].—**beauty.** With a pun on *booty* [s.c.]. The sentence means little more than "Do not allow us, who do good service on the highway by night, to be called thieves in plain terms when the day dawns."—**Let us be:** i.e., let us be called.—**Diana:** the moon goddess and the goddess of maidens.—**Minions:** favourites, darlings. —**of good government:** well-governed—i.e., well-behaved.—**countenance:** with a pun on *countenance* in the sense of "authority," "authorization."— **steal:** go stealthily, rob.[s.c.] 24–30. **it holds well:** what you say about our being "governed by the moon" proves to be consistent with the facts of the case.—**for proof:** for instance; for example.—**with swearing 'Lay by':** by calling upon the traveller (with an oath) to "hand over." *Lay by* is, literally, "lay aside," "lay down your luggage."—**'Bring in':** a call to the wine-waiter at the tavern.—**the ladder:** the ladder from the gallows platform to the *ridge*—the horizontal crossbar which formed the top of the structure. The culprit had to climb the ladder with the noose about his neck. Then it was pulled away from under him, or he was thrown off by the hangman, or, if he was especially courageous, he took the leap himself. We should remember that the punishment for robbery was hanging. 46. **the tavern:** the Boar's Head in Eastcheap. **Hybla:** a mountain (and a town) in Sicily, famous in ancient times for its honey. —**my old lad of the castle.** The character now dubbed Falstaff was called Sir John Old-castle in the play as originally written. See Introduction. A "lad of the castle" was a slang term for a "roisterer."—**a buff jerkin:** a close-fitting jacket of buff-coloured leather, such as sheriff's officers wore.—**of durance:** of durable material. There was a kind of cloth called *durance*. There is a pun on *in durance,* i.e., in confinement. 35. **quips:** witticisms.—**quiddities:** literally, "subtle definitions." The quiddity (*quidditas*) of a thing is "that which it really is," its "what-ness." Cf. the phrase "I know what's what." Here Falstaff uses the word in the general sense of "a smart saying," "a fine-spun or subtle jest." 38. **a reckoning:** an accounting.

FAL.	No; I'll give thee thy due, thou hast paid all there.	40

PRINCE. Yea, and elsewhere, so far as my coin would stretch; and where it would not, I have used my credit.

FAL. Yea, and so us'd it that, were it not here apparent that thou art heir apparent—But I prithee, sweet wag, shall there be gallows standing in England when thou art king? and resolution thus fubb'd as it is with the rusty curb of old father antic the law? Do not thou, when thou art king, hang a thief.

PRINCE. No; thou shalt. *—either hang theif or be hung as theif* (handwritten)

FAL. Shall I? O rare! By the Lord, I'll be a brave judge.   49

PRINCE. Thou judgest false already. I mean, thou shalt have the hanging of the thieves and so become a rare hangman.

FAL. Well, Hal, well; and in some sort it jumps with my humor as well as waiting in the court, I can tell you.

PRINCE. For obtaining of suits?

FAL. Yea, for obtaining of suits, whereof the hangman hath no lean wardrobe. 'Sblood, I am as melancholy as a gib-cat or a lugg'd bear.

PRINCE. Or an old lion, or a lover's lute.

FAL. Yea, or the drone of a Lincolnshire bagpipe.

PRINCE. What sayest thou to a hare, or the melancholy of Moor Ditch?   59

FAL. Thou hast the most unsavoury similes, and art indeed the most comparative, rascalliest, sweet young prince. But, Hal, I prithee trouble me no more with vanity. I would to God thou and I knew where a commodity of good names were to be bought. An old lord of the Council rated me the other day in the street about you, sir, but I

43–46. **here apparent...heir apparent.** *Here* and *heir* are both emphatic. This pun is so outrageous that Falstaff runs away from it without finishing his sentence, changing the subject with a hasty "But." The *heir apparent* is the "manifest and certain heir to the throne"—the King's eldest son. 45–46. **resolution:** the resolute courage shown by robbers.—**fubb'd.** A variant of *fobb'd*: "foiled"; "made of no effect"; "thwarted"—literally, "made a fool of."—**with:** by.—**antic:** buffoon. 49. **brave:** fine, magnificent. 50–51. **have.** Emphatic.—**hangman:** executioner. 52. **in some sort:** in some ways.—**jumps with:** accords with; suits.—**humor:** fancy. 54–55. **suits.** A pun on (1) suits (petitions) to the King for some substantial mark of royal favor and (2) suits of clothes. The clothes of the person executed were a perquisite of the executioner. 56. **'Sblood:** God's blood—an oath by the blood of Christ.—**gib-cat:** a tomcat. *Gib* (a short form for *Gilbert*) was a common name for a cat of either sex. "As melancholy as a cat" was an old proverbial comparison. —**a lugg'd bear.** The slow lumbering gait of a bear gives one the impression of surly reluctance or weary discontent. 58. **the drone...bagpipe:** the dismal sound of the drone (bass pipe) of a bagpipe. 59. **a hare.** A hare sitting in its form was a symbol of melancholy.—**Moor Ditch.** A notoriously filthy ditch or open sewer just outside the city wall. It received drainage from the marshes called Moorfields. 61. **comparative:** adept at abusive comparisons[s.c.]—**vanity:** vain worldly matters. Cf. *Ecclesiastes*, xii, 8. 63. **a commodity:** a supply.[s.c.] 64. **rated:** berated, scolded.

mark'd him not; and yet he talk'd very wisely, but I regarded him not;
and yet he talk'd wisely, and in the street too.   66

PRINCE.   Thou didst well; for wisdom cries out in the streets, and no man
regards it.

FAL.   O, thou hast damnable iteration, and art indeed able to corrupt a saint.
making fun of   Thou hast done much harm upon me, Hal—God forgive thee for
extreme protestant   it! Before I knew thee, Hal, I knew nothing; and now am I, if a man
ism that is black   should speak truly, little better than one of the wicked. I must give over
and white   this life, and I will give it over! By the Lord, an I do not, I am a villain!
I'll be damn'd for never a king's son in Christendom.

PRINCE.   Where shall we take a purse tomorrow, Jack?   75

FAL.   Zounds, where thou wilt, lad! I'll make one. An I do not, call me
villain and baffle me.

PRINCE.   I see a good amendment of life in thee—from praying to purse-taking.

FAL.   Why, Hal, 'tis my vocation, Hal. 'Tis no sin for a man to labor in his
vocation.   80
Enter Poins.

Poins! Now shall we know if Gadshill have set a match. O, if men were
to be saved by merit, what hole in hell were hot enough for him? This
is the most omnipotent villain that ever cried 'Stand!' to a true man.

PRINCE.   Good morrow, Ned.   84

POINS.   Good morrow, sweet Hal. What says Monsieur Remorse? What says
Sir John Sack and Sugar? Jack, how agrees the devil and thee about thy
soul, that thou soldest him on Good Friday last for a cup of Madeira
and a cold capon's leg?

67–68. **wisdom...regards it.** "Wisdom crieth without; she uttereth her voice in the streets...I have
stretched out my hand, and no man regarded" (*Proverbs,* i, 20, 24). 69. **damnable iteration:** a
damnable trick of repeating what one says and giving it a satirical twist. 72–73. **give over this life:**
give up this way of living.—**an:** if.—**a villain:** a low fellow; no gentleman. 76. **Zounds.** The same as
'*Swounds.* Literally (as still understood in Shakespeare's time) this is a tremendous oath: "By God's
wounds"—i.e., the wounds which Christ suffered on the cross. It is significant that the Folio omits
"Zounds," in accordance with the statute of 1606 forbidding profanity on the stage.—**An:** if. 77. **baffle
me.** To *baffle* is to "degrade from knighthood." The offender was stripped of his armor and the shield
with his coat of arms was turned upside down. Sometimes he was hanged in effigy, heels up. 79–80.
'**Tis no sin...vocation.** A more or less proverbial perversion of a Biblical text: "Let every man abide
in the same calling wherein he was called" (*1 Corinthians,* vii, 20). 81–83. **Gadshill.** Gadshill is a hill
on the Kentish road near Rochester. It was notorious for highway robberies. —**set a match:** made an
appointment for a robbery—literally, for a match game. Gadshill is the *setter.*—**if men were to be
saved by merit.** Falstaff has in mind the doctrine that no man deserves salvation; if saved, men owe it
to the grace of God.—'**Stand!'** Stand and deliver!—the highwayman's phrase in accosting the traveller
whom he holds up.—**true:** honest. 84. **Good morrow:** good morning. 85–86. **Monsieur Remorse:** i.e.,
compassion, pity—the last name one would expect to be applied to a robber.—**Sack and Sugar.** It was
the fashion to sweeten sherry with a touch of sugar.

PRINCE.   Sir John stands to his word, the devil shall have his bargain; for he was
never yet a breaker of proverbs. He will give the devil his due.   90

POINS.   Then art thou damn'd for keeping thy word with the devil.

PRINCE.   Else he had been damn'd for cozening the devil.

POINS.   But, my lads, my lads, tomorrow morning, by four o'clock early, at
Gadshill! There are pilgrims going to Canterbury with rich offerings,
and traders riding to London with fat purses. I have vizards for you
all; you have horses for yourselves. Gadshill lies tonight in Rochester.
I have bespoke supper tomorrow night in Eastcheap. We may do it as
secure as sleep. If you will go, I will stuff your purses full of crowns; if
you will not, tarry at home and be hang'd!   99

FAL.   Hear ye, Yedward: if I tarry at home and go not, I'll hang you for
going.

POINS.   You will, chops?

FAL.   Hal, wilt thou make one?

PRINCE.   Who, I rob? I a thief? Not I, by my faith.   104

FAL.   There's neither honesty, manhood, nor good fellowship in thee, nor
thou cam'st not of the blood royal if thou darest not stand for ten
shillings.

PRINCE.   Well then, once in my days I'll be a madcap.

FAL.   Why, that's well said.

PRINCE.   Well, come what will, I'll tarry at home.   110

FAL.   By the Lord, I'll be a traitor then, when thou art king.

PRINCE.   I care not.

POINS.   Sir John, I prithee, leave the Prince and me alone. I will lay him down
such reasons for this adventure that he shall go.   114

---

89. **a breaker of proverbs:** one who violates the doctrine that proverbs teach. The Prince goes on to
explain that Falstaff is a lost soul, since the proverb bids him "give the devil his due." This old saying
(quoted in *Henry V*) is merely an emphatic assertion of the principle that we should give *everybody*
his due. 91. **keeping thy word.** Poins implies that Falstaff has long ago renounced his fealty to God
and given his soul to Satan by becoming a confirmed sinner. 92. **cozening:** cheating. Thus the Prince
maintains that Falstaff's soul is lost in any case. 93–99. **But.** Poins turns aside from jesting and comes
down to the serious business of the moment.—**early:** i.e., four o'clock in the morning.—**to Canterbury:**
to the shrine of Saint Thomas of Canterbury (Thomas à Becket) in the cathedral.—**vizards:** masks.—
lies: lodges.—**in Rochester:** on the road from London to Canterbury.—**bespoke:** engaged, ordered.—
Eastcheap: in London—the site of Falstaff's favourite tavern, kept by Dame Quickly. The name means
"East Market." 100. **Yedward:** Edward.—**hang you:** have you hanged. 102. **chops:** you fat-chops; you
fat-jawed fellow. 105–106. **honesty:** honor. Falstaff has in mind the proverb: "There's honor among
thieves."—**royal.** A royal was a gold coin worth ten shillings. There is a pun on *stand for:* (1) "be valued
at"; (2) "take your stand on the road to obtain (by robbery)." 108. **once in my days:** for once in my
life.

FAL.   Well, God give thee the spirit of persuasion and him the ears of
            profiting, that what thou speakest may move and what he hears may
            be believed, that the true prince may (for recreation sake) prove a false
            thief; for the poor abuses of the time want countenance. Farewell; you
            shall find me in Eastcheap.

[handwritten margin note: awareness of the inevitable change that's coming]

PRINCE.   Farewell, thou latter spring! farewell, All-hallown summer!   120
                                                        [*Exit Falstaff.*]

POINS.   Now, my good sweet honey lord, ride with us tomorrow. I have a jest
            to execute that I cannot manage alone. Falstaff, Bardolph, Peto, and
            Gadshill shall rob those men that we have already waylaid; yourself and
            I will not be there; and when they have the booty, if you and I do not
            rob them, cut this head off from my shoulders.   125

PRINCE.   How shall we part with them in setting forth?

POINS.   Why, we will set forth before or after them and appoint them a place
            of meeting, wherein it is at our pleasure to fail; and then will they
            adventure upon the exploit themselves; which they shall have no
            sooner achieved, but we'll set upon them.   130

PRINCE.   Yea, but 'tis like that they will know us by our horses, by our habits,
            and by every other appointment, to be ourselves.

POINS.   Tut! our horses they shall not see—I'll tie them in the wood; our
            vizards we will change after we leave them; and, sirrah, I have cases of
            buckram for the nonce, to immask our noted outward garments.   135

PRINCE.   Yea, but I doubt they will be too hard for us.

POINS.   Well, for two of them, I know them to be as true-bred cowards as ever
            turn'd back; and for the third, if he fight longer than he sees reason, I'll
            forswear arms. The virtue of this jest will be the incomprehensible lies
            that this same fat rogue will tell us when we meet at supper: how thirty,
            at least, he fought with; what wards, what blows, what extremities he
            endured; and in the reproof of this lies the jest.   142

115–118. **Well, God give thee,** etc. Falstaff assumes the manner of a preacher exhorting his
congregation.—**the poor abuses...countenance:** i.e., lack encouragement from men of high rank.
Falstaff parodies the regular complaint that good causes are not properly encouraged by the nobility.
120. **thou latter spring:** i.e., thou old fellow who still hast the feelings of a youngster. The idea is
repeated in the next phrase; for *All-hallown* is All-hallows (All Saints) day, i.e., November first. *All-
hallown summer,* then, is what we now call "Indian summer." 122. **Bardolph, Peto.** The Quartos and
Folios have "Haruey, Rossill." Probably Harvey and Russell were the actors who took the parts of
Bardolph and Peto. 127–130. In *The Famous Victories* the Prince takes a leading part in the attack.
Shakespeare has so modified the adventure as to relieve him of the guilt of downright highway robbery.
131–132. **habits:** clothes, attire.—**appointment:** accoutrement. 134–135. **sirrah.** A form of *sir,* used
in familiar address. Poins is treating the Prince as a comrade.—**cases of buckram:** close fitting suits of
buckram—coarse cloth stiffened with glue.—**for the nonce:** for the occasion; for the express purpose.
The phrase is a modification of *for then once* ("for that one time").—**noted:** well-known. 136. **doubt:**
fear. 137–142. **for:** as for.—**forswear arms:** renounce the profession of arms.—**incomprehensible:**
unlimited, infinite.—**wards:** parries. —**extremities:** extreme hazards.—**reproof:** disproof, refutation.

Hal (Keith Baxter) delivering his "I know you all" soliloquy with Falstaff (Orson Welles) in the rear of the frame. (Welles's *Chimes at Midnight*)

PRINCE.   Well, I'll go with thee. Provide us all things necessary and meet me
tonight in Eastcheap. There I'll sup. Farewell.

POINS.   Farewell, my lord   *Exit.* 145

PRINCE.   I know you all, and will awhile uphold†
The unyok'd humor of your idleness.
Yet herein will I imitate the sun, *say* *imitating | the prince*
Who doth permit the base contagious clouds
To smother up his beauty from the world, *when ne's most needed* 150
That, when he please again to be himself, *he will emerge*
Being wanted, he may be more wond'red at *from the clouds*
By breaking through the foul and ugly mists
Of vapors that did seem to strangle him.
If all the year were playing holidays,   155
To sport would be as tedious as to work;
But when they seldom come, they wish'd-for come,
And nothing pleaseth but rare accidents.

146. **will awhile...idleness:** will continue to obey that fancy for freedom from restraint which leads
me to share in your folly. 148. **sun:** This symbol of royalty often plays upon "son"—a natural pun used
throughout the play. [s.c.] 149. **contagious.** Pestilence was thought to be generated in fog, mist, and
cloud. 158. **rare accidents:** things that happen seldom.

†   Welles's film transforms Hal's famous soliloquy into something more complicated as Falstaff, in
the rear of the frame, is a silent witness to the prince's remarks, though it is hard to judge how
much he actually hears or comprehends of Hal's pledge to reform. [s.c.]

So, when this loose behaviour I throw off
And pay the debt I never promised, *— i didn't sign up for this*   160
By how much better than my word I am,
By so much shall I falsify men's hopes;
And, like bright metal on a sullen ground,
religious My reformation, glitt'ring o'er my fault,
language Shall show more goodly and attract more eyes   *brighter by contrast* 165
Than that which hath no foil to set it off.   *he's gonna seem even*
redeem "the debt" I'll so offend to make offence a skill,   *better bc of the drastic*
through Hotspur Redeeming time when men think least I will.   *change*   *Exit.*

biggest threat
and prove legitimacy?   SCENE III. [*London. The Palace.*]

Enter the King, Northumberland, Worcester, Hotspur, Sir Walter Blunt, *with others.*

KING.   My blood hath been too cold and temperate,
        Unapt to stir at these indignities,
        And you have found me, for accordingly
        You tread upon my patience; but be sure
        I will from henceforth rather be myself,   5
        Mighty and to be fear'd, than my condition,
        Which hath been smooth as oil, soft as young down,
        And therefore lost that title of respect
        Which the proud soul ne'er pays but to the proud.

WOR.   Our house, my sovereign liege, little deserves   10
        The scourge of greatness to be us'd on it—
        And that same greatness too which our own hands
        Have holp to make so portly.

NORTH. My lord—

KING.   Worcester, get thee gone; for I do see   15
        Danger and disobedience in thine eye.
        O, sir, your presence is too bold and peremptory,

---

162. **hopes:** expectations. 163. **a sullen ground:** a dull-coloured background. 164. **fault:** with a pun on the geological image Hal develops here. [S.C.] 165. **show more goodly:** appear more beautiful. 166. **foil:** a leaf (Latin *folium*) of metal, used in the setting for a gem.—**to set it off:** to make it appear the brighter by contrast. 167. **to:** as to.—**a skill:** a clever device. 168. **Redeeming time:** making up for time wasted. Cf. *Ephesians* 5: 15-16. Note that in the next scene Hotspur commits himself to redeeming honor, setting up the clash between timing and honor which distinguishes the Hal-Hotspur competition. [S.C.]

SCENE III
The interval between this scene, again at the king's court in London, and scene 1 cannot be exactly determined. Perhaps a week or two has elapsed.[S.C.] 2, 3. **Unapt:** not ready; slow.—**found me:** found me out. 5, 6. **myself:** i.e., a king.—**my condition:** my natural disposition. 13. **holp:** helped.—**portly:** stately. **Danger:** defiance. 17. **péremptory:** commanding, imperious.

And majesty might never yet endure

weakness The moody frontier of a servant brow.

You have good leave to leave us. When we need   20

Your use and counsel, we shall send for you.   *Exit Worcester.*

You were about to speak.

NORTH.   Yea, my good lord.

Those prisoners in your Highness' name demanded

Which Harry Percy here at Holmedon took,

Were, as he says, not with such strength denied   25

As is delivered to your Majesty.

Either envy, therefore, or misprision

Is guilty of this fault, and not my son.

HOT.   My liege, I did deny no prisoners.

But I remember, when the fight was done,   30

When I was dry with rage and extreme toil,

Breathless and faint, leaning upon my sword,

Came there a certain lord, neat and trimly dress'd,

Fresh as a bridegroom; and his chin new reap'd

Show'd like a stubble land at harvest home.   35

He was perfumed like a milliner,

And 'twixt his finger and his thumb he held

A pouncet box, which ever and anon

He gave his nose, and took't away again;

Who therewith angry, when it next came there,   40

Took it in snuff; and still he smil'd and talk'd;

And as the soldiers bore dead bodies by,

He call'd them untaught knaves, unmannerly,

To bring a slovenly unhandsome corse

Betwixt the wind and his nobility.   45

With many holiday and lady terms

He questioned me, amongst the rest demanded

18, 19. **majesty...brow:** a king has never yet been able to bear the sight of a servant who showed him a frowning forehead. A *frontier* is the outwork of a fortification. **delivered:** reported.—**envy...or misprision:** malice or mistake (on the part of your informant). **dry:** thirsty.—**éxtreme.** Such dissyllabic adjectives are regularly accented on the first syllable when an accented syllable comes next in the verse. 33. **neat:** exquisite in his attire; foppish. 34, 35. **new reap'd.** Hotspur means merely that the beard had been newly trimmed—in contrast with the rough beard of a soldier.—**Show'd:** looked. 36. **milliner.** This trade was carried on by men in old times. 38. **A pouncet box:** a pomander. This was a small box or jar filled with some perfume or aromatic substance and having a perforated cover. It was used for refreshment or to protect one's olfactory nerve from disagreeable odors. **therewith angry:** angry at having had the pouncet box taken away.—**took it in snuff:** showed that he (the nose) was offended. The pun is obvious. To *take* anything *in snuff* is to "resent it strongly." The phrase comes from the way in which some persons show anger—by drawing in the breath audibly through the nostrils. —**still:** always. 44, 45. **corse:** corpse.—**his nobility:** his noble self. 47. **He questioned me.** This seems to mean not merely "interrogated me" but "insisted on talking to me"; for to *question* often signifies "talk."

My prisoners in your Majesty's behalf.
I then, all smarting with my wounds being cold,
To be so pest'red with a popingay,   50
Out of my grief and my impatience
Answer'd neglectingly, I know not what—
He should, or he should not; for he made me mad
To see him shine so brisk, and smell so sweet,
And talk so like a waiting gentlewoman   55
Of guns and drums and wounds—God save the mark!—
And telling me the sovereignest thing on earth
Was parmacity for an inward bruise;
And that it was great pity, so it was,
This villanous saltpetre should be digg'd   60
Out of the bowels of the harmless earth,
Which many a good tall fellow had destroy'd
So cowardly; and but for these vile guns,
He would himself have been a soldier.
This bald unjointed chat of his, my lord,   65
I answered indirectly, as I said,
And I beseech you, let not his report
Come current for an accusation
Betwixt my love and your high majesty.

BLUNT.   The circumstance considered, good my lord,   70
          Whate'er Lord Harry Percy then had said
          To such a person, and in such a place,
          At such a time, with all the rest retold,
          May reasonably die, and never rise
          To do him wrong, or any way impeach   75
          What then he said, so he unsay it now.

KING.   Why, yet he doth deny his prisoners,
          But with proviso and exception,
          That we at our own charge shall ransom straight

---

50. **To be:** at being. The infinitive depends on *smarting*.—**pest'red with a popingay:** annoyed by the constant chatter of this senseless fop. 51. **Out of:** as the result of.—**grief:** pain (from my wounds). 52. **neglectingly:** negligently; without thinking what I said—whether "yes" or "no." 56. **God save the mark!** God avert the evil omen! 57. **sovereignest thing:** best of all remedies. 58. **parmacity:** spermaceti, a waxy solid derived from the oil of whales, a substance used in perfumes. 62. **tall:** sturdy and valiant. 63, 64. **guns:** cannon. The point he made was that warfare is no longer a glorious thing, as it was in the old days of hand-to-hand fighting before gunpowder was invented. 66. **indirectly.** Hotspur uses this word as a synonym for "neglectingly." 68. **Come current:** be accepted at its face value. 70–73. **circumstance.** Modern English would use the plural.—**had said:** may have said.—**all the rest:** all the other details that he has mentioned. 75, 76. **To do him wrong:** to do him an injury.—**impeach:** make subject to blame.—**so:** provided that. 77, 78. **yet.** The emphatic *yet*: "after all," "when all is said and done." —**deny his prisoners:** refuse to surrender his prisoners to me.—**But:** except.—**proviso and exception.** Synonymous. 79. **we:** I, the King. —**straight:** straightway, immediately.

His brother-in-law, the foolish Mortimer;   80
Who, on my soul, hath wilfully betray'd
The lives of those that he did lead to fight
Against that great magician, damn'd Glendower,
Whose daughter, as we hear, the Earl of March
Hath lately married. Shall our coffers, then,   85
Be emptied to redeem a traitor home?
Shall we buy treason? and indent with fears
When they have lost and forfeited themselves?
No, on the barren mountains let him starve!
For I shall never hold that man my friend   90
Whose tongue shall ask me for one penny cost
To ransom home revolted Mortimer.

HOT.   Revolted Mortimer?
He never did fall off, my sovereign liege,
But by the chance of war. To prove that true   95
Needs no more but one tongue for all those wounds,
Those mouthed wounds, which valiantly he took
When on the gentle Severn's sedgy bank,
In single opposition hand to hand,
He did confound the best part of an hour   100
In changing hardiment with great Glendower.
Three times they breath'd, and three times did they drink,
Upon agreement, of swift Severn's flood;
Who then, affrighted with their bloody looks,
Ran fearfully among the trembling reeds   105
And hid his crisp head in the hollow bank,
Bloodstained with these valiant combatants.
Never did base and rotten policy
Color her working with such deadly wounds;
Nor never could the noble Mortimer   110
Receive so many, and all willingly.

80–84. **brother-in-law...Mortimer...Earl of March.** Hotspur's wife was the older sister of Edmund de Mortimer, captured by Glendower and confused by Shakespeare, perhaps intentionally, with Edmund Mortimer, Richard II's heir.[s.c.] 86. **redeem...home:** ransom and bring home.—**a traitor:** because now in league with Glendower. 87, 88. **indent with fears:** make an indenture (a contract) with objects of fear (persons whom we have reason to fear).—**lost and forfeited.** Synonymous: "when they have delivered themselves up to the enemy." 92. **revolted:** rebellious. 97. **Those mouthed wounds.** That wounds are mouths is a figure of speech which appealed strongly to Shakespeare. 100–101. **confound:** spend.—**In changing hardiment:** in contending hand to hand—showing their valor in single combat; literally, "in exchanging valor." 102–105. **breath'd:** stopped to take breath. **with:** by.—**fearfully:** in fright; in a panic. The river god was terrified by their fierce looks. 106. **crisp:** curled. Alluding to the rippling surface of a stream. 108–109. **policy:** political trickery. Spoken with scornful emphasis. *Policy* is regularly applied (like *political* and *politician*) to chicanery in public affairs. **Color her working:** give a false show of patriotism. 110. **Nor never.** Such double negatives are used to strengthen the negation.

	Then let not him be slandered with revolt.	

KING.　Thou dost belie him, Percy, thou dost belie him!
He never did encounter with Glendower.
I tell thee　　　　　　　　　　　　　　　　　　　　　　115
He durst as well have met the devil alone
As Owen Glendower for an enemy.
Art thou not asham'd? But, sirrah, henceforth
Let me not hear you speak of Mortimer.
Send me your prisoners with the speediest means,　　120
Or you shall hear in such a kind from me
As will displease you. My Lord Northumberland,
We license your departure with your son.—
Send us your prisoners, or you will hear of it.
　　　　　　　　　　　　　　Exeunt King, [Blunt, and Train].

HOT.　And if the devil come and roar for them,　　　　125
I will not send them. I will after straight
And tell him so; for I will ease my heart,
Albeit I make a hazard of my head.

NORTH.　What, drunk with choler? Stay, and pause awhile.
Here comes your uncle.

　　　　　　　　　　　Enter Worcester.

HOT.　　　　　　　　Speak of Mortimer?　　　　　　130
Zounds, I will speak of him, and let my soul
Want mercy if I do not join with him!
Yea, on his part I'll empty all these veins,
And shed my dear blood drop by drop in the dust,
But I will lift the downtrod Mortimer　　　　　　135
As high in the air as this unthankful king,
As this ingrate and cank'red Bolingbroke.— *refuses to call him king)*

NORTH.　Brother, the King hath made your nephew mad.

WOR.　Who struck this heat up after I was gone?

---

112. **with revolt:** by an accusation of having revolted from his allegiance to the English king. Hotspur is repudiating the King's phrase "revolted Mortimer" (l. 92). 113. **dost belie him:** does not tell the truth about him. 116. **alone:** in single combat. 118. **sirrah.** See 1.2.135, note. Here used in scorn. **speak.** Emphatic: "Let me not hear you even mention his name." 121. **kind:** fashion, manner, way. 123. **license your departure:** give you our permission to depart. 125. **An if:** if. *An* is *and*. This passage shows how *an* came to be used in this sense. 126. **I will...straight:** I'll follow him at once. 128. **Albeit:** even if. 129. **choler:** anger. 130. **Speak.** Emphatic. 131. **Zounds.** See 1.2.76, note. [s.c.] 132. **join.** Emphatic. 135. **But:** but that—i.e., if *that* is necessary in order to; if *that* is the only means by which I can. 137. **ingrate:** thankless. A strong synonym for "ungrateful."—**cank'red:** malignant. From *canker*, "an eating sore," "a cancer or ulcer."—**Bolingbroke.** Percy refuses to call him King and uses the family name.

HOT.	He will (forsooth) have all my prisoners;	140
	And when I urg'd the ransom once again	
	Of my wive's brother, then his cheek look'd pale,	
	And on my face he turn'd an eye of death,	
	Trembling even at the name of Mortimer.	
WOR.	I cannot blame him. Was not he proclaim'd	145
	By Richard that dead is, the next of blood?	
NORTH.	He was; I heard the proclamation.	
	And then it was when the unhappy King	
	(Whose wrongs in us God pardon!) did set forth	
	Upon his Irish expedition;	150
	From whence he intercepted did return	
	To be depos'd, and shortly murdered.	
WOR.	And for whose death we in the world's wide mouth	
	Live scandaliz'd and foully spoken of.	
HOT.	But soft, I pray you. Did King Richard then	155
	Proclaim my brother Edmund Mortimer	
	Heir to the crown?	
NORTH.	He did; myself did hear it.	
HOT.	Nay, then I cannot blame his cousin king,	
	That wish'd him on the barren mountains starve.	
	But shall it be that you, that set the crown	160
	Upon the head of this forgetful man,	
	And for his sake wear the detested blot	
	Of murtherous subornation—shall it be	
	That you a world of curses undergo,	
	Being the agents or base second means,	165
	The cords, the ladder, or the hangman rather?	
	O, pardon me that I descend so low	

140. **forsooth.** Literally, "truly," but used parenthetically as a mere interjection of ironical impatience. 141. **urg'd:** mentioned—not, pressed or insisted on. 142. **wive's.** The old form of the genitive, still heard in rapid speech. 143. **an eye of death:** a deathly eye; an eye of mortal fear. 145, 146. **proclaim'd... the next of blood:** proclaimed by Richard II as his nearest relative and therefore as heir to the crown. Shakespeare follows Holinshed. In fact, however, it was the father of Edmund, Earl of March—Roger, the fourth Earl—who was recognized by Parliament (in 1385) as heir presumptive. 149. **Whose... pardon!** And for the wrongs we did him may God pardon us! 151. **intercepted:** interrupted—by the return of the banished Bolingbroke to England and the civil war that ensued. 152. **depos'd.** Richard's abdication took place on September 30, 1399. He died (or was murdered) in the following January. 155. **soft:** wait a moment,—literally, slowly. 156. **my brother.** Roger, Earl of March, was Hotspur's brother-in-law. Edmund, the next Earl, was Roger's son. 159. **wish'd him...starve.** See line 89. 162, 163. **detested:** detestable, hateful.—**murtherous subornation:** procurement of murder. 165. **second means.** Synonymous with *agents.* 166. **ladder:** means of ascent but also an instrument of the hangman. Hotspur realizes that in helping Bolingbroke to rise, his family has become the king's now hated hatchet men. [S.C.]

detractors before
king)

To show the line and the predicament
Wherein you range under this subtle king!
Shall it for shame be spoken in these days, *haven't been recognized* 170
Or fill up chronicles in time to come, *for his help putting into*
That men of your nobility and power *power*
Did gage them both in an unjust behalf
(As both of you, God pardon it! have done)
To put down Richard, that sweet lovely rose,   175
And plant this thorn, this canker, Bolingbroke?
And shall it in more shame be further spoken
That you are fool'd, discarded, and shook off
By him for whom these shames ye underwent?
No! yet time serves wherein you may redeem   180
Your banish'd honours and restore yourselves
Into the good thoughts of the world again;
Revenge the jeering and disdain'd contempt
Of this proud king, who studies day and night
To answer all the debt he owes to you   *economic language*   185
Even with the bloody payment of your deaths.   *leverage*
Therefore I say—

WOR.   Peace, cousin, say no more;   *they think they*
And now I will unclasp a secret book,   *can remove him*
And to your quick-conceiving discontents
I'll read you matter deep and dangerous,   190
As full of peril and adventurous spirit
As to o'erwalk a current roaring loud
On the unsteadfast footing of a spear.

HOT.   If he fall in, good night, or sink or swim!
Send danger from the east unto the west,   195
So honor cross it from the north to south,
And let them grapple. O, the blood more stirs
To rouse a lion than to start a hare!

---

168. the line: the rank.—predicament: category. 169. Wherein you range: in which you rank—are classed.—under: under the rule of. 173. gage: pledge, stake.—them both: both their nobility and their power.—in an unjust behalf: in behalf of an unjust claim. 175, 176. rose...canker. The garden rose and the wild rose (thorn rose, dog rose, canker) are contrasted, to the disadvantage of the wild flower. 183. Revenge: and may take vengeance for.—disdain'd: disdainful. 185. answer: pay, discharge. 189. to your quick-conceiving discontents: to your discontented state of mind, which will be on the alert to catch the meaning.—discontents. Abstract nouns are often pluralized when more than one person is referred to. 194. If he fall in...swim! If such a man fall in—why then, if he sinks we must wish him good-night, for he has shown himself a brave adventurer.—or sink or swim: whether he sinks or swims,—literally, let him sink or let him swim. The phrase is proverbial to express indifference to the outcome or to describe one who risks everything in one desperate act ("the last resort"). 196. So: provided that.—cross it: cross its path.

NORTH. Imagination of some great exploit   *self-control*
Drives him beyond the bounds of patience.   200

HOT. By heaven, methinks it were an easy leap
To pluck bright honor from the pale-fac'd moon,   — *idea that you can*
Or dive into the bottom of the deep,   *claim honor*
Where fadom line could never touch the ground,
And pluck up drowned honor by the locks,   — *or succumb to stealing it*   205
So he that doth redeem her thence might wear   *↳ high road or low*
Without corrival all her dignities;   *road*
But out upon this half-fac'd fellowship!   — *refusal to share — arrogance*

WOR. He apprehends a world of figures here,
But not the form of what he should attend.   210
Good cousin, give me audience for a while.

HOT. I cry you mercy.

WOR.   Those same noble Scots
That are your prisoners—

HOT.   I'll keep them all.
By God, he shall not have a Scot of them!
No, if a Scot would save his soul, he shall not.   215
I'll keep them, by this hand!

WOR.   You start away.
And lend no ear unto my purposes.
Those prisoners you shall keep.

HOT.   Nay, I will! That's flat!
He said he would not ransom Mortimer,
Forbade my tongue to speak of Mortimer,   220
But I will find him when he lies asleep,
And in his ear I'll holloa "Mortimer."
Nay;
I'll have a starling shall be taught to speak
Nothing but "Mortimer," and give it him   225
To keep his anger still in motion.

WOR. Hear you, cousin, a word.

---

200. **patience:** self-control. 204. **fadom line:** sounding line.—**fadom.** Because the depth is always reported in *fathoms.* 205. **pluck:** pull. 206. **So:** provided that; if only.—**redeem:** rescue. 207. **corrival:** sharer, associate. 208. **this half-fac'd fellowship!** *Fellowship* is scornfully emphatic: "this miserable necessity of sharing one's honor with others!"—**out upon:** a curse upon; away with.—**half-fac'd:** miserable,—literally, "thin-faced," "cadaverous." 209, 210. **apprehends:** conceives; sees in his mind's eye.—**figures:** figures of speech.—**the form:** the correct figure; the true meaning.—**attend:** attend to; give his mind to. 212. **I cry you mercy:** I beg your pardon. 216. **by this hand.** An idiomatic oath. 217. **my purposes:** my talk; what I say. 218. **I will.** *Will* is emphatic. 220. **to speak:** even to speak. **still:** ever, always.

HOT.   All studies here I solemnly defy
         Save how to gall and pinch this Bolingbroke;
         And that same sword-and-buckler Prince of Wales—   230
         But that I think his father loves him not
         And would be glad he met with some mischance,
         I would have him poisoned with a pot of ale.

WOR.   Farewell, kinsman. I will talk to you
         When you are better temper'd to attend.   235

NORTH.   Why, what a wasp-stung and impatient fool
         Art thou to break into this woman's mood,
         Tying thine ear to no tongue but thine own!

HOT.   Why, look you, I am whipp'd and scourg'd with rods,
         Nettled, and stung with pismires when I hear   240
         Of this vile politician, Bolingbroke.
         In Richard's time—what do you call the place?—
         A plague upon it! it is in Gloucestershire—
         'Twas where the madcap Duke his uncle kept—
         His uncle York—where I first bow'd my knee   245
         Unto this king of smiles, this Bolingbroke—
         'Sblood!
         When you and he came back from Ravenspurgh—

NORTH.   At Berkeley Castle.

HOT.   You say true.   250
         Why, what a candy deal of courtesy
         This fawning greyhound then did proffer me!
         Look, "when his infant fortune came to age,"
         And "gentle Harry Percy," and "kind cousin"—
         O, the devil take such cozeners!—God forgive me!   255
         Good uncle, tell your tale, for I have done.

228, 229. **All studies:** all my pursuits in life; all my interests.—**defy:** renounce.—**gall and pinch:**
annoy, torment. *Gall* is, literally, to "rub the skin off"—and so, to "irritate." 230. **sword-and-buckler.**
In Shakespeare's time the rapier and dagger had replaced the sword and buckler as the weapons of a
gentleman, and sword and buckler had come to be the arms carried by a servant or a person of low rank
233. **ale.** Emphatic. Hotspur implies that the Prince never drinks wine with gentlemen, but associates
only with low fellows whose drink is ale. 234, 235. **Farëwell:** fare ye well.—**better temper'd:** in a more
favourable humor. 236. **wasp-stung:** nervous and irritable. 238. **Tying thine ear...won:** listening to
nothing that is said by others but giving attention only to your own talk. 240. **pismires:** ants. 241.
politician. Common in this contemptuous sense. 242–247. Hotspur is so impatient that he cannot
stop long enough to let his memory work. 244. **kept:** resided. 247. **'Sblood.** See 1.2.56 note. 248.
Ravenspurgh: on the coast of Yorkshire. 249. **At Berkeley Castle.** Northumberland patiently supplies
the name. He knows that he must let Hotspur's excitement run its course. 254. **gentle:** noble—as in
gentleman. 255. **cozeners:** cheats. An unescapable pun. —**God forgive me!** Thus Hotspur begs pardon
for his wild talk and his refusal to listen.

WOR.	Nay, if you have not, to it again.
	We will stay your leisure.
HOT.	I have done, i' faith.
WOR.	Then once more to your Scottish prisoners.

Deliver them up without their ransom straight,   260
And make the Douglas' son your only mean
For powers in Scotland; which, for divers reasons
Which I shall send you written, be assur'd
Will easily be granted. [*To Northumberland*] You, my lord,
Your son in Scotland being thus employ'd,   265
Shall secretly into the bosom creep
Of that same noble prelate well-belov'd,
The Archbishop.

HOT.   Of York, is it not?

WOR.   True; who bears hard
His brother's death at Bristow, the Lord Scroop.   270
I speak not this in estimation,
As what I think might be, but what I know
Is ruminated, plotted, and set down,
And only stays but to behold the face
Of that occasion that shall bring it on.   275

HOT.   I smell it. Upon my life, it will do well.

NORTH.   Before the game is afoot thou still let'st slip.

HOT.   Why, it cannot choose but be a noble plot.
And then the power of Scotland and of York
To join with Mortimer, ha?

WOR.   And so they shall.   280

HOT.   In faith, it is exceedingly well aim'd.

WOR.   And 'tis no little reason bids us speed,
To save our heads by raising of a head;

257, 258. **to it again...leisure:** Start again and keep on. We'll wait until you have a spare moment to listen to us.—**i' faith.** Emphatic. 259. **once more to:** to return to the subject—your Scottish prisoners. 260–262. **straight:** straightway, immediately.—**the Douglas' son:** Mordake. —**mean: means.—powers:** troops. 270. **bears hard:** strongly resents.—**Bristow:** Bristol.—**the Lord Scroop:** William Scrope, Earl of Wiltshire, executed for treason in 1399. Holinshed erroneously represents him as the Archbishop's brother, and Shakespeare follows Holinshed. 271. **in estimation:** as a matter of conjecture. 274. **but** emphasizes the sense of *only.* 275. **occasion:** opportunity. 276. **do well:** succeed. 277. **Before...slip:** You're always letting the dogs loose before the game we are hunting has started to run. 278. **cannot choose but be:** cannot help being. 279–280. **the power:** the armed forces. —**ha?** The interrogative interjection *huh?* 281. **aim'd:** planned, projected. 283. **a head:** an armed force, an army.

	For, bear ourselves as even as we can,	
	The King will always think him in our debt,	285
	And think we think ourselves unsatisfied,	
	Till he hath found a time to pay us home.	
	And see already how he doth begin	
	To make us strangers to his looks of love.	
HOT.	He does, he does! We'll be reveng'd on him.	290
WOR.	Cousin, farewell. No further go in this	
	Than I by letters shall direct your course.	
	When time is ripe, which will be suddenly,	
	I'll steal to Glendower and Lord Mortimer,	
	Where you and Douglas, and our pow'rs at once,	295
	As I will fashion it, shall happily meet,	
	To bear our fortunes in our own strong arms,	
	Which now we hold at much uncertainty.	
NORTH.	Farewell, good brother. We shall thrive, I trust.	
HOT.	Uncle, adieu. O, let the hours be short	300
	Till fields and blows and groans applaud our sport! *Exeunt.*	

ACT II

SCENE I. [*Rochester. An inn yard.*]

Enter a Carrier *with a lantern in his hand.*

1. CAR.	Heigh-ho! an it be not four by the day, I'll be hang'd. Charles' wain is over the new chimney, and yet our horse not pack'd.—What, ostler!
OST.	[*within*] Anon, anon.

---

284. **bear...can:** no matter how carefully we may conduct ourselves. 285. **in our debt:** for the help we gave him in winning the crown. 287. **home:** thoroughly, completely, in full. This sense comes from the idea of a *home thrust,* a sword thrust that reaches a vital spot. 293. **suddenly:** immediately. 295. **our pow'rs at once:** all our forces together. 299. **thrive:** be successful. 301. **fields:** battlefields.
ACT II. SCENE I.
The scene takes place early in the morning at an inn-yard somewhere on the London-Canturbury road. Stage direction: **Carrier:** a person who transports merchandise. 1. **Heigh-ho!** A long yawning sigh.—**four by the day:** four o'clock in the morning.—**Charles' wain:** an old name for the group of stars which we usually call "the Dipper." *Charles' wain* means "the wagon or chariot of Charlemagne (Charles the Great)." It is a corruption of *carl's* (churl's, countryman's) *wain.* 3. **Anon:** presently; in a moment; coming. The regular reply to a call for a waiter or attendant.

1. CAR.   I prithee, Tom, beat Cut's saddle, put a few flocks in the point. Poor
           jade is wrung in the withers out of all cess.   5

           Enter another Carrier.

2. CAR.   Peas and beans are as dank here as a dog, and that is the next way to
           give poor jades the bots. This house is turned upside down since Robin
           Ostler died.

1. CAR.   Poor fellow never joyed since the price of oats rose. It was the death of
           him.   10

2. CAR.   I think this be the most villanous house in all London road for fleas. I
           am stung like a tench.

1. CAR.   Like a tench? By the mass, there is ne'er a king christen could be better
           bit than I have been since the first cock.

2. CAR.   Why, they will allow us ne'er a jordan, and then we leak in your
           chimney, and your chamber-lye breeds fleas like a loach.   16

1. CAR.   What, ostler! come away and be hang'd! come away!

2. CAR.   I have a gammon of bacon and two razes of ginger, to be delivered as
           far as Charing Cross.

1. CAR.   God's body! the turkeys in my pannier are quite starved. What, ostler!
           A plague on thee! hast thou never an eye in thy head? Canst not hear?
           An 'twere not as good deed as drink to break the pate on thee, I am a
           very villain. Come, and be hang'd! Hast no faith in thee?
           Enter *Gadshill.*

GADS.   Good morrow, carriers. What's o'clock?   25

1. CAR.   I think it be two o'clock.

4–5. **beat:** i.e., in order to soften the saddle.—**Cut:** the horse with a docked tail.—**flocks:** wisps of
wool.—**in the point:** the point of the pack-saddle.—**jade:** nag.—**wrung:** sore from having the skin
rubbed off by the saddle.—**the withers:** the ridge between a horse's shoulders. —**out of all cess:**
beyond all account; excessively. 6–8. **Peas and beans.** Used as food for horses—a cheap substitute for
oats.—**dank:** damp.—**as a dog:** a common comparison.—**next:** nearest; quickest.—**the bots:** worms
in the stomach of a horse—**house:** inn.—**Robin:** a familiar form (a so-called diminutive) of *Robert*.
11–12. **a tench:** a kind of spotted fish. 13–14. **By the mass.** A common oath.—**a king christen:** a
Christian king. The Carrier implies that kings have the best of everything.—**the first cock.** The times
of cockcrow were conventionally fixed as follows: first cock, midnight; second cock 3, A.M. . 15–16.
a jordan: a chamber pot.—**chimney:** fireplace [s.c.]—**chamber-lye:** urine.—**a loach:** a kind of fish,
which the Carrier supposes is infested by parasites. 17. **come away:** come along. 18. **a gammon of
bacon:** a leg of bacon; a ham.—**razes:** roots. Ginger, a favourite spice in old times, was imported and
handled in the form of large roots. 19. **Charing Cross.** A village at some distance from London on the
way to Westminster. The growth of the city has absorbed it since Shakespeare's time. 20–23. **God's
body!** An oath by the body of Christ —**as good a deed as drink:** as to take a drink. An old humorous
comparison. —**to break the pate on thee:** of thee. To *break* one's *head* means merely to "break the skin
of the head" so as to draw blood,—not to "fracture the skull."—**villain.** A general term of contempt.—
faith: trustworthiness.

GADS.   I prithee lend me thy lantern to see my gelding in the stable.

1. CAR.   Nay, by God, soft! I know a trick worth two of that, i' faith.

GADS.   I pray thee lend me thine.

2. CAR.   Ay, when? canst tell? Lend me thy lantern, quoth he? Marry, I'll see
thee hang'd first!   31

GADS.   Sirrah carrier, what time do you mean to come to London?

2. CAR.   Time enough to go to bed with a candle, I warrant thee. Come,
neighbour Mugs, we'll call up the gentlemen. They will along with
company, for they have great charge.   *Exeunt [Carriers].*   35

GADS.   What, ho! chamberlain!

Enter Chamberlain.

CHAM.   At hand, quoth pickpurse.

GADS.   That's even as fair as—"at hand, quoth the chamberlain"; for thou
variest no more from picking of purses than giving direction doth from
laboring: thou layest the plot how.   40

CHAM.   Good morrow, Master Gadshill. It holds current that I told you
yesternight. There's a franklin in the Wild of Kent hath brought
three hundred marks with him in gold. I heard him tell it to one of
his company last night at supper—a kind of auditor; one that hath
abundance of charge too, God knows what. They are up already and
call for eggs and butter. They will away presently.   46

GADS.   Sirrah, if they meet not with Saint Nicholas' clerks, I'll give thee this
neck.

CHAM.   No, I'll none of it. I pray thee keep that for the hangman; for I know
thou worshippest Saint Nicholas as truly as a man of falsehood may.   50

GADS.   What talkest thou to me of the hangman? If I hang, I'll make a fat pair
of gallows; for if I hang, old Sir John hangs with me, and thou knowest

---

28. **soft!** wait a moment! don't be in a hurry! —**a trick...that:** namely, *not* to lend thee my lantern. 30–
31. **Ay, when?** canst tell? An ironical phrase for a refusal. —**quoth he?** Often used in scornful repetition
of what one has said.—**Marry.** See 1.2.18, note. **Sirrah.** See 1.2.35, note. **Time enough...candle:** Either
before dark or after dark. A humorously evasive answer. The Carriers are shrewdly suspicious of Gadshill.
34–35. **They will along with company:** They wish to travel with companions for safety's sake.—**great
charge:** a large amount of money; or, in a more general sense, valuable baggage. 36. **chamberlain:** the
man who has charge of guests' rooms at an inn. 37. **At hand, quoth pickpurse:** "Here I am, close by,"
as the pickpocket said. An old slang phrase. 38. **That's even as fair as:** That's just as correct an answer
as. 41. **holds current:** proves to be correct information. 42–46. **a franklin:** a freeholder—not quite a
gentleman in rank.—**the Wild of Kent:** the Weald (Forest) of Kent, a rich agricultural district, once
wooded.—**marks.** A mark was two thirds of a pound sterling.—**auditor:** an officer who looks after
public accounts.—**charge:** luggage.—**eggs and butter.** Cf. 1.2.15–16.—**presently:** at once. 47. **Saint
Nicholas' clerks:** disciples of Old Nick; robbers, highwaymen. 49. **I'll none of it:** I don't care for it; I
have no use for it.

he is no starveling. Tut! there are other Troyans that thou dream'st not of, the which for sport sake are content to do the profession some grace; that would (if matters should be look'd into) for their own credit sake make all whole. I am joined with no foot landrakers, no long-staff sixpenny strikers, none of these mad mustachio purple-hued maltworms; but with nobility and tranquillity, burgomasters and great oneyers, such as can hold in, such as will strike sooner than speak, and speak sooner than drink, and drink sooner than pray; and yet, zounds, I lie; for they pray continually to their saint, the commonwealth, or rather, not pray to her, but prey on her, for they ride up and down on her and make her their boots. *royal are thieves too*   63

CHAM.   What, the commonwealth their boots?
            Will she hold out water in foul way?

GADS.   She will, she will! Justice hath liquor'd her. We steal as in a castle, cocksure. We have the receipt of fernseed, we walk invisible.

CHAM.   Nay, by my faith, I think you are more beholding to the night than to fernseed for your walking invisible.

GADS.   Give me thy hand. Thou shalt have a share in our purchase, as I am a true man.   71

CHAM.   Nay, rather let me have it, as you are a false thief.

GADS.   Go to; "homo" is a common name to all men. Bid the ostler bring my

---

53. **Troyans:** Trojans—a slang term for "roisterers," "sports." 56–63. **foot landrakers:** fellows that wander about the country on foot; vagabond footpads.—**long-staff sixpenny strikers:** low thieves, armed only with long cudgels, who will hold up a traveller for sixpence.—**mustachio purple-hued malt-worms:** ale-drinkers whose long mustaches are stained purple by the beer they soak them in. —**nobility and tranquillity:** noblemen who live at their ease.—**great oneyers:** great ones. —**can hold in:** know how to keep their own counsel; are trustworthy comrades.—**speak sooner than drink:** call upon a traveller to "stand and deliver"—and are even more ready to do so than they are to take a drink.—**their boots:** their booty; their profit. The Chamberlain proceeds to make an easy pun on *boots*. 65. **in foul way:** in a miry road. 66. **liquor'd:** greased. Gadshill continues the pun on *boots.*—**as in a castle.** An idiomatic phrase for "in perfect safety." Gadshill alludes to the name of his leader—Sir John Oldcastle. This was the name of the knight in the play as first written. *Falstaff* was a substitute made before it was printed. See Introduction. 67. **the receipt of fernseed:** the formula which enables one to find the seed of ferns (which is almost invisible). It was an old belief that to carry fernseed gathered on St. John's Eve (June 23) made one invisible. 68. **beholding:** beholden, obliged, indebted. 70. **purchase:** booty. Cf. 3.3.30: "there's no purchase in money." 71. **true:** honest. 73. **"homo"...men:** and so we'll omit the adjective ("true" or "false") and let my pledge stand in the form "as I am a man." Gadshill is quoting the definition of a *common* noun in Lily's *Latin Grammar*—the standard primary text book in Shakespeare's day and long after. Gadshill implies that he is a *true man* (a *real* man) even if he is not *true* (honest). 74. **muddy:** muddle-headed, stupid. But the Chamberlain has proved himself a match for Gadshill in this duel of wits.

gelding out of the stable. Farewell, you muddy knave.   *Exeunt.*

SCENE II. [*The highway near Gad's Hill.*]

Enter Prince *and* Poins.

POINS.   Come, shelter, shelter! I have remov'd Falstaff's horse, and he frets like a gumm'd velvet.

PRINCE.   Stand close.   [*They step aside.*]

Enter Falstaff.

FAL.   Poins! Poins, and be hang'd! Poins!

PRINCE.   [*comes forward*] Peace, ye fat-kidney'd rascal! What a brawling dost thou keep!   6

FAL.   Where's Poins, Hal?

PRINCE.   He is walk'd up to the top of the hill.
I'll go seek him.   [*Steps aside.*]

FAL.   I am accurs'd to rob in that thief's company. The rascal hath removed my horse and tied him I know not where. If I travel but four foot by the squire further afoot, I shall break my wind. Well, I doubt not but to die a fair death for all this, if I scape hanging for killing that rogue. I have forsworn his company hourly any time this two-and-twenty years, and yet I am bewitch'd with the rogue's company. If the rascal have not given me medicines to make me love him, I'll be hang'd. It could not be else. I have drunk medicines. Poins! Hal! A plague upon you both! Bardolph! Peto! I'll starve ere I'll rob a foot further. An 'twere not as good a deed as drink to turn true man and to leave these rogues, I am the veriest varlet that ever chewed with a tooth. Eight yards of uneven ground is threescore and ten miles afoot with me, and the stony-hearted villains know it well enough. A plague upon it when thieves cannot be true one to another! (*They whistle.*) Whew! A plague

---

SCENE II
The location is the highway near Gad's Hill. 2, 3. **he frets like a gumm'd velvet.** A punning comparison. Velvet of inferior quality was treated with gum to give the pile an appearance of firmness. Such gummed velvet *fretted* quickly when used, i.e., the pile wore away, leaving bare spots. Silk (especially taffeta) was gummed to make it seem firm. —**close:** in concealment. 11, 12. **by the squire:** measured by the carpenter's "square."—**break my wind:** pant and wheeze like a wind-broken horse. 16–25. **medicines:** love potions, philtres. Falstaff is speaking whimsically, but belief in such magical prescriptions was almost universal in Shakespeare's time.—**as good a deed as drink.** See 2.1.22, note.—**true:** honest.—**varlet:** low rascal, scamp.—**when thieves...another.** Falstaff is thinking of the proverb, "There is honor among thieves." He gives the principle a comic application, as if fidelity were more to be expected of thieves than of honest men. —**Whew!** Falstaff tries to whistle in reply.

upon you all! Give me my horse, you rogues! give me my horse and be
hang'd! 25

PRINCE. [*comes forward*] Peace, ye fat-guts! Lie down, lay thine ear close to the
ground, and list if thou canst hear the tread of travellers.

FAL. Have you any levers to lift me up again, being down? 'Sblood, I'll not
bear mine own flesh so far afoot again for all the coin in thy father's
exchequer. What a plague mean ye to colt me thus? 30

PRINCE. Thou liest; thou art not colted, thou art uncolted.

FAL. I prithee, good Prince Hal, help me to my horse, good king's son.

PRINCE. Out, ye rogue! Shall I be your ostler?

FAL. Go hang thyself in thine own heir-apparent garters! If I be ta'en,
I'll peach for this. An I have not ballads made on you all, and sung
to filthy tunes, let a cup of sack be my poison. When a jest is so
forward—and afoot too—I hate it. 37

Enter Gadshill, [Bardolph *and* Peto *with him*].

GADS. Stand!

FAL. So I do, against my will.

POINS. [*comes forward*] O, 'tis our setter. I know his voice. Bardolph, what
news? 41

BAR. Case ye, case ye! On with your vizards! There's money of the King's
coming down the hill; 'tis going to the King's exchequer.

FAL. You lie, ye rogue! 'Tis going to the King's tavern.

GADS. There's enough to make us all. 45

FAL. To be hang'd.

PRINCE. Sirs, you four shall front them in the narrow lane; Ned Poins and I will
walk lower. If they scape from your encounter, then they light on us.

PETO. How many be there of them?

30, 31. **colt:** trick.—**uncolted:** deprived of thy horse. 32. **I prithee.** Falstaff assumes a wheedling,
coaxing tone, which he changes abruptly when the Prince refuses his request. 33. **Out.** An interjection
of scornful rejection: "Away with you!" The modern slang phrase "Get out!" is a direct descendant.
34. **heir-apparent garters.** An allusion to the Order of the Garter, in which Hal was enrolled as heir
apparent. 35–37. **peach:** give information.—**for this:** in revenge for this trick you've played on me.—
ballads. Ballads were the news sheets of Shakespeare's time and later. Every important or sensational
event was instantly worked up in verse. Ballads were printed on single sheets (as broadsides) and were
sung and peddled about the streets. —**and afoot too:** and especially when it keeps me on my feet. 39.
against my will: for I should prefer to be on horseback. 40. **setter.** Gadshill is the *setter*—that member
of the gang who collects information and makes arrangements for robberies. The dog called a *setter* gets
his name for a similar reason. 42. **ye:** yourselves.—**vizards:** masks. 45. **make us all:** make the fortunes
of us all. 48. **us.** Emphatic. Falstaff is not a coward: he is merely grumbling, and he soon recovers his
temper.

GADS.	Some eight or ten.	50
FAL.	Zounds, will they not rob us?	
PRINCE.	What, a coward, Sir John Paunch?	
FAL.	Indeed, I am not John of Gaunt, your grandfather; but yet no coward, Hal.	
PRINCE.	Well, we leave that to the proof.	55
POINS.	Sirrah Jack, thy horse stands behind the hedge. When thou need'st him, there thou shalt find him. Farewell and stand fast.	
FAL.	Now cannot I strike him, if I should be hang'd.	
PRINCE.	[*aside to Poins*] Ned, where are our disguises?	
POINS.	[*aside to Prince*] Here, hard by.	60
	Stand close. [*Exeunt Prince and Poins.*]	
FAL.	Now, my masters, happy man be his dole, say I. Every man to his business.†	

Enter the Travellers.

TRAVELLER.	Come, neighbour.	
	The boy shall lead our horses down the hill;	65
	We'll walk afoot awhile and ease our legs.	
THIEVES.	Stand!	
TRAVELLER.	Jesus bless us!	
FAL.	Strike! down with them! cut the villains' throats! Ah, whoreson caterpillars! bacon-fed knaves! they hate us youth. Down with them! fleece them!	71
TRAVELLER.	O, we are undone, both we and ours for ever!	

---

53. **John of Gaunt.** The Duke of Lancaster; so called because he was born at Gaunt (Ghent). Falstaff's pun was "destiny unshunnable"; but it did not lack personal application, for Prince Hal was tall and thin. Cf. the exchange of epithets between the two in 2.4.191–195. 55. **the proof:** the test. 61. **close:** in hiding. 62. **my masters.** Used in the vocative like "gentlemen" now-a-days.—**happy man be his dole:** may it be his lot (that which is *dealt* out to him by fate) to be a fortunate man! The *his* has no personal reference. Falstaff simply quotes an old formula for "Good luck!" or "May the best man win!" 69. **villains:** low fellows—a general term of abuse and contempt, like *knaves* in lines 70, 73. 70. **caterpillars.** The regular term for "parasites" or persons who enrich themselves at others' expense—especially for corrupt officers of the government. 72. **undone:** ruined.

---

†   This is a moment when actor and director often tip their hand about their approach to Falstaff. Welles, for instance, plays the robbery scene simply for laughs; his Falstaff is benign. But Barry Stanton, in the ESC production, is a tougher character and his Falstaff gives one of the downed victims a swift kick in the groin. [s.c.]

FAL.   Hang ye, gorbellied knaves, are ye undone? No, ye fat chuffs; I would
your store were here! On, bacons, on! What, ye knaves! young men
must live. You are grand-jurors, are ye? We'll jure ye, faith!   75

Here they rob and bind them.

Exeunt.

Enter the Prince *and* Poins [*in buckram suits*].

PRINCE.   The thieves have bound the true men. Now could thou and I rob the
thieves and go merrily to London, it would be argument for a week,
laughter for a month, and a good jest for ever.

POINS.   Stand close! I hear them coming.   [*They stand aside.*]

Enter the Thieves *again.*

FAL.   Come, my masters, let us share, and then to horse before day. An the
Prince and Poins be not two arrant cowards, there's no equity stirring.
There's no more valor in that Poins than in a wild duck.   82

PRINCE.   Your money!

As they are sharing, the Prince *and* Poins *set upon them. They all run away, and*
Falstaff, *after a blow or two, runs away too, leaving the booty behind them.*

POINS.   Villains!

PRINCE.   Got with much ease. Now merrily to horse.   85
The thieves are scattered, and possess'd with fear
So strongly that they dare not meet each other.
Each takes his fellow for an officer.
Away, good Ned. Falstaff sweats to death
And lards the lean earth as he walks along.   90
Were't not for laughing, I should pity him.

POINS.   How the rogue roar'd!   *Exeunt.*

---

73. **gorbellied:** fat-paunched, potbellied.—**chuffs:** rich curmudgeons, misers. 74. **your store:** all you
possess.—**bacons:** fat fellows. 75. **grand-jurors.** Men of some property were regularly chosen to serve
on the grand jury.—**We'll jure ye.** *Jure* means nothing in particular. Such plays on words are still
common in humorous threats. 76–77. **true:** honest.—**argument:** a subject of conversation; something
to talk about. 81. **there's no equity stirring:** there's no such thing as correct judgment in the world—
neither I nor anybody else can judge a man's character.

Hotspur (Norman Rodway), in his bath, reading the letter from a potential ally who refuses to join the rebellion, while his wife Kate looks on from above. (Welles's *Chimes at Midnight*)

SCENE III. [*Warkworth Castle.*]

Enter Hotspur *solus, reading a letter.* —someone back in your [?] / [?] are they opening battle [handwritten]

HOT.   "But, for mine own part, my lord, I could be well contented to be there, in respect of the love I bear your house." He could be contented—why is he not then? In respect of the love he bears our house! He shows in this he loves his own barn better than he loves our house. Let me see some more. "The purpose you undertake is dangerous"—Why, that's certain! 'Tis dangerous to take a cold, to sleep, to drink; but I tell you, my lord fool, out of this nettle, danger, we pluck this flower, safety. "The purpose you undertake is dangerous, the friends you have named uncertain, the time itself unsorted, and your whole plot too light for the counterpoise of so great an opposition." Say you so, say you so? I say unto you again, you are a shallow, cowardly hind, and you lie. What a lack-brain is this! By the Lord, our plot is a good plot as ever was laid; our friends true

won't meet up—line on page before [handwritten]

SCENE III

This scene takes place at Warkworth Castle in Northumberland, a stronghold belonging to Percy's father. 1, 2. Shakespeare does not inform us who was Hotspur's correspondent. The last few lines of the speech suggest that he was Dunbar, the Scottish Earl of March, for Holinshed says that he urged the King to attack the rebels before their forces should "too much increase."—**could be well contented:** should be pleased.—**house:** family. 9–12. **unsorted:** unfit.—**for the counterpoise of:** to counterbalance.—**hind:** peasant.

Kate (Michele Dotrice) trying to get news of the impending rebellion from her husband, Hotspur (Tim Pigott-Smith). (BBC-TV)

and constant: a good plot, good friends, and full of expectation; an excellent plot, very good friends. What a frosty-spirited rogue is this! Why, my Lord of York commends the plot and the general course of the action. Zounds, an I were now by this rascal, I could brain him with his lady's fan. Is there not my father, my uncle, and myself; Lord Edmund Mortimer, my Lord of York, and Owen Glendower? Is there not, besides, the Douglas? Have I not all their letters to meet me in arms by the ninth of the next month, and are they not some of them set forward already? What a pagan rascal is this! an infidel! Ha! you shall see now, in very sincerity of fear and cold heart will he to the King and lay open all our proceedings. O, I could divide myself and go to buffets for moving such a dish of skim milk with so honourable an action! Hang him, let him tell the King! we are prepared. I will set forward tonight.[†]   26

Enter his Lady.

14. **full of expectation:** a very promising plot. 15. **my Lord of York:** the Archbishop. 20. **all their letters to meet me:** letters from all of them promising to meet me. 22. **pagan:** because he has no faith in our project. 24. **divide…buffets:** split myself in two and let the two halves have a boxing match.

[†]   In Welles's film Hotspur (Norman Rodway) is reading the letter while taking his bath. He becomes so infuriated at the letter writer's reluctance to join the rebellion that he leaps out of his bath momentarily forgetting his towel. Hotspur is a hot-head but, as Welles and Rodway suggest here, a likeable one who makes us laugh even as we realize that his impatience and intemperance are likely to prove fatal in his confrontation with the king and Hal.

How now, Kate? I must leave you within these two hours.

LADY.   O my good lord, why are you thus alone?‡
For what offence have I this fortnight been
A banish'd woman from my Harry's bed?   *left her bed —*
Tell me, sweet lord, what is't that takes from thee   *too obsessed w/* 30
Thy stomach, pleasure, and thy golden sleep?   *fighting*
Why dost thou bend thine eyes upon the earth,   *(and regaining honor)*
And start so often when thou sit'st alone?
Why hast thou lost the fresh blood in thy cheeks   35
And given my treasures and my rights of thee
To thick-ey'd musing and curs'd melancholy?
In thy faint slumbers I by thee have watch'd,
And heard thee murmur tales of iron wars,
Speak terms of manage to thy bounding steed,   40
Cry "Courage! to the field!" And thou hast talk'd
Of sallies and retires, of trenches, tents,
Of palisadoes, frontiers, parapets,
Of basilisks, of cannon, culverin,
Of prisoners' ransom, and of soldiers slain,   45
And all the currents of a heady fight.
Thy spirit within thee hath been so at war,
And thus hath so bestirr'd thee in thy sleep,
That beads of sweat have stood upon thy brow
Like bubbles in a late-disturbed stream,   50
And in thy face strange motions have appear'd,
Such as we see when men restrain their breath
On some great sudden hest. O, what portents are these?
Some heavy business hath my lord in hand,
And I must know it, else he loves me not.   55

HOT.   What, ho!

---

28 ff. This interview between Percy and his wife may be profitably compared with that between Brutus and Portia. Lady Percy, though apparently rebuffed, learns all that she wishes to know. 32. **stomach:** appetite. 38. **faint:** light—antithetic to *sound and dreamless.* 40. **manage:** manège, horsemanship. 43, 44. **palisadoes:** stakes set up as a defence.—**frontiers:** outworks of a fortification. —**basilisks...cannon...culverin.** Three grades of ordnance. The basilisk was the heaviest, the culverin the lightest. 51. **motions.** This combines the literal sense with the figurative—"emotions." 53. **on some great sudden hest:** when about to undertake some great action to which they are suddenly called.—**porténts:** ominous signs. 54. **heavy.** This combines two meanings: "weighty" and "woeful."

---

‡   In the less than seventy lines exchanged here between Hotspur and Kate, Shakespeare presents a dynamic portrait of a marriage. Kate is as bold, curious, and quick as her husband and she presses him with a heady independence about his plans. In the BBC production, Kate (Michele Dotrice) and Hotspur (Tim Pigott-Smith) begin the scene by sitting next to each other on a series of steps leading up to a long passageway. The scene moves from steps to corridor as their encounter becomes more passionate and physical. [s.c.]

                                                    [*Enter a Servant.*]
                    Is Gilliams with the packet gone?

SERV.   He is, my lord, an hour ago.

HOT.   Hath Butler brought those horses from the sheriff?

SERV.   One horse, my lord, he brought even now.

HOT.   What horse? A roan, a crop-ear, is it not?   60

SERV.   It is, my lord.

HOT.   That roan shall be my throne.
            Well, I will back him straight. O esperance!
            Bid Butler lead him forth into the park.   [*Exit Servant.*]

LADY.   But hear you, my lord.

HOT.   What say'st thou, my lady?   65

LADY.   What is it carries you away?

HOT.   Why, my horse, my love—my horse!

LADY.   Out, you mad-headed ape!
            A weasel hath not such a deal of spleen
            As you are toss'd with. In faith.   70
            I'll know your business, Harry; that I will!
            I fear my brother Mortimer doth stir
            About his title and hath sent for you
            To line his enterprise; but if you go—

HOT.   So far afoot, I shall be weary, love.   75

LADY.   Come, come, you paraquito, answer me
            Directly unto this question that I ask.
            In faith, I'll break thy little finger, Harry,
            An if thou wilt not tell me all things true.

HOT.   Away,   80
            Away, you trifler! Love? I love thee not;
            I care not for thee, Kate. This is no world
            To play with mammets and to tilt with lips.

---

63. **esperance!** "Esperance ma comforte" ("Hope is my stay," "my reliance") was the motto of the Percys, and "esperance" was their watchword and battle cry. 69. **spleen.** What we now-a-days call "nervousness" or "excitability." The spleen was supposed to be the organ whose action causes sudden impulse, caprice, fits of irritation, irritability, etc. 72–74. **my brother.** Lady Percy was the elder sister to Edward de Mortimer, but the fifth Earl of March, whom Richard II named as his heir to the throne, was her nephew. Shakespeare conflates these two figures following Holinshed. [s.c.].—**doth stir:** is in action.—**title:** i.e., to the crown.—**line:** to support. 76. **paraquito:** a talkative parrot. [s.c.] 81. **Love?** Hotspur in his reply jumps back to what Lady Percy had said before he interrupted her by calling the servant (l. 68). This absent-minded trick of speech is burlesqued by Prince Hal in 2.4.81 ff. 83. **mammets:** dolls—like you.—**to tilt with lips.** Play kissing games. [s.c.]

	We must have bloody noses and crack'd crowns,	
	And pass them current too. Gods me, my horse!	85
	What say'st thou, Kate? What wouldst thou have with me?	
LADY.	Do you not love me? do you not indeed?	
	Well, do not then; for since you love me not,	
	I will not love myself. Do you not love me?	
	Nay, tell me if you speak in jest or no.	90
HOT.	Come, wilt thou see me ride?	
	And when I am a-horseback, I will swear	
	I love thee infinitely. But hark you, Kate:	
	I must not have you henceforth question me	
	Whither I go, nor reason whereabout.	95
	Whither I must, I must; and to conclude,	
	This evening must I leave you, gentle Kate.	
	I know you wise; but yet no farther wise	
	Than Harry Percy's wife; constant you are,	
	But yet a woman; and for secrecy,	100
	No lady closer, for I well believe	
	Thou wilt not utter what thou dost not know,	
	And so far will I trust thee, gentle Kate.	
LADY.	How? so far?	
HOT.	Not an inch further. But hark you, Kate:	105
	Whither I go, thither shall you go too;	
	Today will I set forth, tomorrow you.	
	Will this content you, Kate?	
LADY.	It must of force. *Exeunt.*	

---

85. **pass them current:** make people take them as valid payment; make them the regular currency. The pun depends on the fact that a coin would not pass if it had a crack extending from the edge to a point inside the circle that surrounded the monarch's head or other device. The old coins had no milled edges and cracked easily. —**Gods me.** A contraction of "God save me!" 95. **whereabout:** about what; on what business. 102. **Thou wilt not utter what thou dost not know.** A stock jest for nearly two thousand years. 108. **of force:** perforce. Lady Percy, though she pretends to be not quite satisfied, has won the day. She knows that Hotspur is to ride away tomorrow, and he has not denied that her guess (ll. 84–86) is right.

SCENE IV. [*Eastcheap. The Boar's Head Tavern.*]

Enter Prince *and* Poins.

PRINCE.   Ned, prithee come out of that fat-room and lend me thy hand to laugh
a little.

POINS.   Where hast been, Hal?   3

PRINCE.   With three or four loggerheads amongst three or fourscore hogsheads.
I have sounded the very bass-string of humility. Sirrah, I am sworn
brother to a leash of drawers and can call them all by their christen
names, as Tom, Dick, and Francis. They take it already upon their
salvation that, though I be but Prince of Wales, yet I am the king
of courtesy; and tell me flatly I am no proud Jack like Falstaff, but a
Corinthian, a lad of mettle, a good boy (by the Lord, so they call me!),
and when I am King of England I shall command all the good lads
in Eastcheap. They call drinking deep, dying scarlet; and when you
breathe in your watering, they cry "hem!" and bid you play it off. To
conclude, I am so good a proficient in one quarter of an hour that I
can drink with any tinker in his own language during my life. I tell
thee, Ned, thou hast lost much honor that thou wert not with me in
this action. But, sweet Ned—to sweeten which name of Ned, I give
thee this pennyworth of sugar, clapp'd even now into my hand by
an under-skinker, one that never spake other English in his life than
"Eight shillings and sixpence," and "You are welcome," with this shrill
addition, "Anon, anon, sir! Score a pint of bastard in the Half-moon,"
or so. But, Ned, to drive away the time till Falstaff come, I prithee do

---

SCENE IV
The place of this scene is fixed as Eastcheap by Prince Hal's words in 1.2.144. In *The Famous Victories*
the Prince and his companions go to "the olde Tauerne in East-cheape" after the robbery. The
Boar's Head was a well-known tavern, and that it was Falstaff's favourite inn is clear from *2 Henry
IV.* 1. **fat-room:** vat-room. *Fat* (Anglo-Saxon *fæt*) is the old form of the word *vat*. 4–6. **loggerheads:**
blockheads.—**sworn brother.** The phrase comes from the old institution of brotherhood in arms. Two
or more persons would take a solemn oath to stand by each other on all occasions as if they were "born
brothers."—**drawers:** the waiters who draw and serve the wine. 6–12. **christen.** See 2.1.13.—**take it...
salvation:** take the oath "as we hope to be saved."—**Jack:** fellow.—**a Corinthian:** a sport. *Trojan* and
Ephesian were also cant words for a "boon companion."—**a lad of mettle:** a fellow of the right sort.—**a
good boy.** Cf., in modern slang: "one o' the boys." *Good boys* (like *good fellows*) was a cant term for
"thieves." 13, 14. **when you breathe in your watering:** when you stop to take breath in your drinking.
In drinking with a friend one was expected to drain his glass or tankard in one draught. *Watering* was a
slang word for "drinking."—**hem!** The sound of clearing one's throat. Sometimes it is an expression of
contempt; sometimes a call of encouragement to activity or vigorous effort. —**play it off:** drink it off.
17. **action:** encounter. A synonym for *battle*. Hal mock's Hotspur's language here by applying it to his
gamesmanship with Falstaff and the tavern lads.[s.c.] 18. **pennyworth of sugar.** The drawers kept sugar
folded up in papers, ready to be delivered to those who called for sack. 19. **under-skinker:** an assistant
wine-waiter. To *skink* is to "pour" (cf. German *schenken*). 21. **Anon:** immediately. The conventional
answer of a servant or waiter when summoned.—**bastard:** a kind of sweet wine.—**the Half-moon.**
Rooms in inns had names instead of numbers.

thou stand in some by-room while I question my puny drawer to what end he gave me the sugar; and do thou never leave calling "Francis!" that his tale to me may be nothing but "Anon!" Step aside, and I'll show thee a precedent.   26

POINS.   Francis!

PRINCE.   Thou art perfect.

POINS.   Francis!   [*Exit Poins.*]

Enter [Francis, *a*] *Drawer.*

FRAN.   Anon, anon, sir.—Look down into the Pomgarnet, Ralph.   30

PRINCE.   Come hither, Francis.

FRAN.   My lord?

PRINCE.   How long hast thou to serve, Francis?

FRAN.   Forsooth, five years, and as much as to—

POINS.   [*within*] Francis!   35

FRAN.   Anon, anon, sir.

PRINCE.   Five year! by'r Lady, a long lease for the clinking of pewter. But, Francis, darest thou be so valiant as to play the coward with thy indenture and show it a fair pair of heels and run from it?

FRAN.   O Lord, sir, I'll be sworn upon all the books in England I could find in my heart—   41

POINS.   [*within*] Francis!

FRAN.   Anon, sir.

PRINCE.   How old art thou, Francis?

FRAN.   Let me see. About Michaelmas next I shall be—   45

POINS.   [*within*] Francis!

FRAN.   Anon, sir. Pray stay a little, my lord.

PRINCE.   Nay, but hark you, Francis. For the sugar thou gavest me—'twas a pennyworth, was't not?

FRAN.   O Lord! I would it had been two!   50

---

26. **a precedent:** a joke worth imitating. 30. **Look down into:** go down and look into.—**Pomgarnet:** Pomegranate. 33. **to serve:** i.e., as an apprentice. The full term of apprenticeship at any trade was seven years. 37. **by'r Lady:** by our Lady—an oath by the Virgin Mary.—**for the clinking of pewter:** a long service to learn such a trade! 39. **thy indenture:** the contract under which you serve your master. 40. **books:** bibles. 45. **Michaelmas:** the feast of Michael the Archangel (September 29): an important holiday and one of the four quarter-days in the calendar.

PRINCE.   I will give thee for it a thousand pound. Ask me when thou wilt, and thou shalt have it.

POINS.   [*within*] Francis!

FRAN.   Anon, anon.

PRINCE.   Anon, Francis? No, Francis; but tomorrow, Francis; or, Francis, a Thursday; or indeed, Francis, when thou wilt. But Francis—   56

FRAN.   My lord?

PRINCE.   Wilt thou rob this leathern-jerkin, crystal-button, not-pated, agate-ring, puke-stocking, caddis-garter, smooth-tongue, Spanish-pouch—

FRAN.   O Lord, sir, who do you mean?   60

PRINCE.   Why then, your brown bastard is your only drink; for look you, Francis, your white canvas doublet will sully. In Barbary, sir, it cannot come to so much.

FRAN.   What, sir?

POINS.   [*within*] Francis!   65

PRINCE.   Away, you rogue! Dost thou not hear them call?

Here they both call him. The Drawer stands amazed, not knowing which way to go.

Enter Vintner.

---

51. **when thou wilt:** any time you wish,—i.e., never. Francis, we may be sure, is not such a fool as to take Prince Hal's promise seriously. He is used to the pranks of sportive gentlemen. 58–59 **rob** Spoken with emphasis and in a tone that startles Francis. After a slight pause, to let the word sink in, the Prince rattles off a description of the innkeeper as fast as he can speak. Francis is too startled to recognize the portrait, and his confusion is made absolute by Prince Hal's reply to his "Who do you mean?"— **leathern-jerkin:** wearing a leather jacket.—**not-pated:** with hair cut short. Gentlemen wore long hair. —**agate-ring:** wearing a seal ring with an agate set in it.—**puke-stocking:** wearing dark-coloured woolen stockings. Gentlemen wore light-coloured silk stockings.—**caddis-garter.** Caddis was a kind of tape. Gentlemen wore elaborate garters of silk or some expensive material, often embroidered and sometimes having a gold clasp. Stockings reached to the knee, where the breeches came to an end. The garter was worn in plain sight.—**Spanish-pouch.** The innkeeper wore some kind of pouch at his girdle to serve as a purse. 61–63. **your.** A lightly spoken *your* (with no personal application); equivalent to the indefinite *this*, which is still in colloquial use. Cf. 2.1.15.—**your only drink:** the only drink worth mentioning; the best of all drinks. —**doublet:** a closefitting jacket.—**In Barbary...much.** The Prince is talking incoherent nonsense to mystify Francis. One is tempted to make sense of it, and perhaps Hal has some thought or other in the back of his mind: "You'd better stick to your trade and learn to serve wine. If you rob your master, you'll become a fugitive. A white doublet like that you are wearing will not keep clean long; and if you take refuge in foreign parts like Barbary, you won't find much use for it there!" 66. **Away, you rogue!** And so this jest with the drawer comes to an end. Sentimental readers here and there feel that the Prince has treated the boy ill; but they need not distress themselves. When Francis grew up and became an innkeeper himself, we may be sure that he often told with intense self-satisfaction how he had once been on intimate terms with Prince Hal.—**amazed:** in a maze; utterly confused; dumbfounded. **Vintner.** Some think this was Dame Quickly's husband (3.3.43) since she was the hostess of the Boar's Head tavern. *Vintner* (literally "wine dealer") sometimes means "innkeeper," "host," "landlord"—sometimes "manager of an inn," "head waiter," or the like. This seems to be the sense here.

VINT.   What, stand'st thou still, and hear'st such a calling? Look to the guests within. [*Exit Francis.*] My lord, old Sir John, with half-a-dozen more, are at the door. Shall I let them in?

PRINCE.   Let them alone awhile, and then open the door. [*Exit Vintner.*] Poins!

POINS.   [*within*] Anon, anon, sir.   71

                                    Enter Poins.

PRINCE.   Sirrah, Falstaff and the rest of the thieves are at the door. Shall we be merry?

POINS.   As merry as crickets, my lad. But hark ye; what cunning match have you made with this jest of the drawer? Come, what's the issue?   75

PRINCE.   I am now of all humors that have showed themselves humors since the old days of goodman Adam to the pupil age of this present twelve o'clock at midnight.

                                                              [*Enter Francis.*]
          What's o'clock, Francis?

FRAN.   Anon, anon, sir.   [*Exit.*] 80

PRINCE.   That ever this fellow should have fewer words than a parrot, and yet the son of a woman! His industry is upstairs and down-stairs, his eloquence the parcel of a reckoning. I am not yet of Percy's mind, the Hotspur of the North; he that kills me some six or seven dozen of Scots at a breakfast, washes his hands, and says to his wife, "Fie upon this quiet life! I want work." "O my sweet Harry," says she, "how many hast thou kill'd today?" "Give my roan horse a drench," says he, and answers "Some fourteen," an hour after, "a trifle, a trifle." I prithee call in Falstaff. I'll play Percy, and that damn'd brawn shall play Dame Mortimer his wife. "Rivo!" says the drunkard. Call in ribs, call in tallow.

          Enter Falstaff, [Gadshill, Bardolph, *and* Peto; Francis *follows with wine*].

POINS.   Welcome, Jack. Where hast thou been?   91

FAL.   A plague of all cowards, I say, and a vengeance too! Marry and amen! Give me a cup of sack, boy. Ere I lead this life long, I'll sew nether-stocks, and mend them and foot them too. A plague of all cowards! Give me a cup of sack, rogue. Is there no virtue extant?*He drinketh.* 95

---

71. **Anon, anon, sir.** Poins is imitating Francis. 74–75. **what cunning match...issue?** What is the clever purpose you have had in playing this game with the drawer? What is to be the outcome? What's the point of it all? Prince Hal informs Poins (and the audience) that there was *no point* except the mere fun of the game itself. 76–77. **I am now of all humours:** Why, it was just a whim of mine. I am in the mood to indulge any fancy that any man has ever had since the creation.—**pupil:** youthful. 83. **parcel of a reckoning:** an item in a bill. 87. **a drench:** a medicinal draught. 89. **brawn:** fat pig. 90. **Rivo!** A shout to encourage drinking. 92–95. **of:** on.—**sack:** a dry wine that was usually fortified and sweetened. [s.c.]—**nether-stocks:** stockings. The *upper stocks* are the breeches.—**Is there no virtue extant?** Is there no manly quality in existence?

PRINCE.   Didst thou never see Titan kiss a dish of butter? Pitiful-hearted butter, that melted at the sweet tale of the sun! If thou didst, then behold that compound.

FAL.   You rogue, here's lime in this sack too! There is nothing but roguery to be found in villanous man. Yet a coward is worse than a cup of sack with lime in it—a villanous coward! Go thy ways, old Jack, die when thou wilt; if manhood, good manhood, be not forgot upon the face of the earth, then am I a shotten herring. There lives not three good men unhang'd in England; and one of them is fat, and grows old. God help the while! A bad world, I say. I would I were a weaver; I could sing psalms or anything. A plague of all cowards I say still!   106

PRINCE.   How now, woolsack? What mutter you?

FAL.   A king's son! If I do not beat thee out of thy kingdom with a dagger of lath and drive all thy subjects afore thee like a flock of wild geese, I'll never wear hair on my face more. You Prince of Wales?   110

PRINCE.   Why, you whoreson round man, what's the matter?

FAL.   Are not you a coward? Answer me to that—and Poins there?

POINS.   Zounds, ye fat paunch, an ye call me coward, by the Lord, I'll stab thee.   114

FAL.   I call thee coward? I'll see thee damn'd ere I call thee coward, but I would give a thousand pound I could run as fast as thou canst. You are straight enough in the shoulders; you care not who sees your back. Call you that backing of your friends? A plague upon such backing! Give me them that will face me. Give me a cup of sack. I am a rogue if I drunk today.   120

PRINCE.   O villain! thy lips are scarce wip'd since thou drunk'st last.

FAL.   All is one for that. (*He drinketh.*) A plague of all cowards still say I.

PRINCE.   What's the matter?

FAL.   What's the matter? There be four of us here have ta'en a thousand pound this day morning.   125

96–98. **Titan:** the sun.—**Pitiful-hearted butter...sun!** Tender-hearted butter that melted into tears at the loving words of the sun! —**If...compound:** if you ever did, then look at Falstaff and you will recognize him as exactly that compound—melting butter. 99. **lime.** Wine was doctored with lime to increase its dryness and make it sparkle in the glass.—**sack too!** Both words are emphasized. *Too* indicates an additional grievance—besides that of which he has been complaining. There is no emphasis on *this.* "You rogue" is addressed to Francis. 101–106. **thy ways:** on thy way. —**a shotten herring:** as thin as a herring that has discharged its roe. —**the while:** the times we live in.—**a weaver.** Weavers were famous singers. Many of them came from the Low Countries and were dissenters—fond of psalm-singing. 108–109. **a dagger of lath:** such as was carried by the Vice—the comic character in the old morality plays. 122. **All is one for that:** That makes no difference.

PRINCE.   Where is it, Jack? Where is it?

FAL.   Where is it? Taken from us it is. A hundred upon poor four of us!

PRINCE.   What, a hundred, man?

FAL.   I am a rogue if I were not at half-sword with a dozen of them two
hours together. I have scap'd by miracle. I am eight times thrust
through the doublet, four through the hose; my buckler cut through
and through; my sword hack'd like a handsaw—*ecce signum*! I never
dealt better since I was a man. All would not do. A plague of all
cowards! Let them speak. If they speak more or less than truth, they are
villains and the sons of darkness.   135

PRINCE.   Speak, sirs. How was it?

GADS.   We four set upon some dozen—

FAL.   Sixteen at least, my lord.

GADS.   And bound them.

PETO.   No, no, they were not bound.   140

FAL.   You rogue, they were bound, every man of them, or I am a Jew else—
an Ebrew Jew.

GADS.   As we were sharing, some six or seven fresh men set upon us—

FAL.   And unbound the rest, and then come in the other.

PRINCE.   What, fought you with them all?   145

FAL.   All? I know not what you call all, but if I fought not with fifty of them,
I am a bunch of radish! If there were not two or three and fifty upon
poor old Jack, then am I no two-legg'd creature.

PRINCE.   Pray God you have not murd'red some of them.   149

FAL.   Nay, that's past praying for. I have pepper'd two of them. Two I am
sure I have paid, two rogues in buckram suits. I tell thee what, Hal—if
I tell thee a lie, spit in my face, call me horse. Thou knowest my old
ward. Here I lay, and thus I bore my point. Four rogues in buckram let
drive at me.

---

129. **at half-sword:** in close combat. 132. *ecce signum:* Latin for "behold the evidence" as Falstaff shows
his hacked sword. [s.c.] 133. **dealt better:** dealt better blows; wielded my sword better. 142. **Ebrew
Jew.** i.e. foresworn. Shakespeare's characters sometimes use the term *Jew* to connote ingratitude and
blasphemy. [s.c.] 151. **paid:** settled with; paid in full.—**buckram.** See 1.2.135, note. 152–153. **call me
horse.** The horse often serves as an example of stupidity.—**my old ward:** my accustomed trick of warding
off a sword stroke. —**Here I lay.** This was the way I stood. Falstaff strikes an attitude and acts the part.
146. At about this point Falstaff (already suspicious) begins to feel pretty sure that the Prince has played
him a trick. To test the matter, and to provide himself with a good answer if his suspicions come true, he
raises the number of his alleged assailants with every breath. He does not expect Hal and Poins to believe
him in these absurdities. Thus he is ready—when the Prince reveals the facts—to retort: "Why, I knew
all that before!" with the implication: "and that's why I gave you such an absurd account of the whole
affair. You might have guessed from my nonsensical story that I didn't expect you to believe me."

PRINCE.	What, four? Thou saidst but two even now.	155
FAL.	Four, Hal. I told thee four.	
POINS.	Ay, ay, he said four.	
FAL.	These four came all afront and mainly thrust at me. I made me no more ado but took all their seven points in my target, thus.	
PRINCE.	Seven? Why, there were but four even now.	160
FAL.	In buckram?	
POINS.	Ay, four, in buckram suits.	
FAL.	Seven, by these hilts, or I am a villain else.	
PRINCE.	[aside to Poins] Prithee let him alone. We shall have more anon.	
FAL.	Dost thou hear me, Hal?	165
PRINCE.	Ay, and mark thee too, Jack.	
FAL.	Do so, for it is worth the list'ning to. These nine in buckram that I told thee of—	
PRINCE.	So, two more already.	
FAL.	Their points being broken—	170
POINS.	Down fell their hose.	
FAL.	Began to give me ground; but I followed me close, came in, foot and hand, and with a thought seven of the eleven I paid.	
PRINCE.	O monstrous! Eleven buckram men grown out of two!	174
FAL.	But, as the devil would have it, three misbegotten knaves in Kendal green came at my back and let drive at me; for it was so dark, Hal, that thou couldst not see thy hand.	
PRINCE.	These lies are like their father that begets them—gross as a mountain, open palpable. Why, thou clay-brain'd guts, thou knotty-pated fool, thou whoreson obscene greasy tallow-catch—	180
FAL.	What, art thou mad? art thou mad? Is not the truth the truth?	

158–159. **afront:** abreast.—**mainly:** strongly.—**target:** buckler. 163. **by these hilts.** The hilt of a sword, consisting of several parts, is often thus designated by a plural. To swear by one's sword was a very old form of oath. —**a villain:** a low fellow; no gentleman. 171. **Down fell their hose.** Poins puns on the word *points*—the name for the tagged laces that attached the hose (the breeches) to the doublet (the jacket). 175–176. **Kendal green.** Kendal in Westmoreland was celebrated for cloth manufacture. 178–180. **gross:** literally, "big," and so "obvious."—**clay-brain'd.** Cf. "muddy" in 2.1.74.—**knotty-pated fool:** blockhead.—**tallow-catch.** Apparently a variant form of *tallow-keech*: a big lump of tallow, rolled up by the butcher to be sent to the chandler—the candle-maker.

PRINCE.   Why, how couldst thou know these men in Kendal green when it was
             so dark thou couldst not see thy hand? Come, tell us your reason.
             What sayest thou to this?   185

POINS.   Come, your reason, Jack, your reason.

FAL.   What, upon compulsion? Zounds, an I were at the strappado or all
             the racks in the world, I would not tell you on compulsion. Give you
             a reason on compulsion? If reasons were as plentiful as blackberries, I
             would give no man a reason upon compulsion, I.   190

PRINCE.   I'll be no longer guilty of this sin; this sanguine coward, this bed-
             presser, this horseback-breaker, this huge hill of flesh—

FAL.   'Sblood, you starveling, you elf-skin, you dried neat's-tongue, you bull's
             pizzle, you stockfish—O for breath to utter what is like thee!—you
             tailor's yard, you sheath, you bowcase, you vile standing tuck!   195

PRINCE.   Well, breathe awhile, and then to it again; and when thou hast tired
             thyself in base comparisons, hear me speak but this.

POINS.   Mark, Jack.

PRINCE.   We two saw you four set on four, and bound them and were masters of
             their wealth. Mark now how a plain tale shall put you down. Then did
             we two set on you four and, with a word, outfac'd you from your prize,
             and have it; yea, and can show it you here in the house. And, Falstaff,
             you carried your guts away as nimbly, with as quick dexterity, and
             roar'd for mercy, and still run and roar'd, as ever I heard bullcalf. What
             a slave art thou to hack thy sword as thou hast done, and then say it
             was in fight! What trick, what device, what starting hole canst thou
             now find out to hide thee from this open and apparent shame?   207

POINS.   Come, let's hear, Jack. What trick hast thou now?

FAL.   By the Lord, I knew ye as well as he that made ye. Why, hear you, my
             masters. Was it for me to kill the heir apparent? Should I turn upon
             the true prince? Why, thou knowest I am as valiant as Hercules; but
             beware instinct. The lion will not touch the true prince. Instinct is a
             great matter. I was now a coward on instinct. I shall think the better

---

187. **the strappado.** A kind of torture in which the victim was drawn up by a rope fastened to his arms
and then let down with a jerk. 189. **reasons.** Pronounced like *raisins.* 191. **sanguine:** full-blooded. The
old physiology ascribed four *humours* (liquids) to the body: blood, phlegm, choler (bile), and melancholy
(black bile). One's temperament depended on the preponderance of one or another of these humours: it
was sanguine, phlegmatic, choleric, or melancholy. A *sanguine coward* would be an unnatural creature,
for a man of "sanguine temperament" was expected to be high-spirited and courageous. 193–195.
Sblood. See 1.2.56, note.—**elf-skin:** skin in which an elf wraps himself.—**stockfish:** salt codfish or
hake.—**standing tuck:** rapier standing on its point. 201. **with a word:** in a word; to make a long story
short.—**outfac'd you from your prize:** deprived you of it by defiant force. 206. **starting hole:** a hole
into which one darts for safety (like a rat or a mouse); a refuge. 210. **my masters.** See 2.2.62, note. 212.
The lion...prince. As King of Beasts the lion was thought to respect royal blood.

of myself, and thee, during my life—I for a valiant lion, and thou for a true prince. But, by the Lord, lads, I am glad you have the money. Hostess, clap to the doors. Watch tonight, pray tomorrow. Gallants, lads, boys, hearts of gold, all the titles of good fellowship come to you! What, shall we be merry? Shall we have a play extempore?

PRINCE.   Content—and the argument shall be thy running away.

FAL.   Ah, no more of that, Hal, an thou lovest me!   220

Enter Hostess.

HOST.   O Jesu, my lord the Prince!

PRINCE.   How now, my lady the hostess?
What say'st thou to me?

HOST.   Marry, my lord, there is a nobleman of the court at door would speak with you. He says he comes from your father.   225

PRINCE.   Give him as much as will make him a royal man, and send him back again to my mother.

FAL.   What manner of man is he?

HOST.   An old man.

FAL.   What doth gravity out of his bed at midnight? Shall I give him his answer?   231

PRINCE.   Prithee do, Jack.

FAL.   Faith, and I'll send him packing.   *Exit.*

PRINCE.   Now, sirs. By'r lady, you fought fair; so did you, Peto; so did you, Bardolph. You are lions too, you ran away upon instinct, you will not touch the true prince; no—fie!   236

BARD.   Faith, I ran when I saw others run.

PRINCE.   Tell me now in earnest, how came Falstaff's sword so hack'd?

PETO.   Why, he hack'd it with his dagger, and said he would swear truth out of England but he would make you believe it was done in fight, and persuaded us to do the like.   241

BARD.   Yea, and to tickle our noses with spear-grass to make them bleed, and then to beslubber our garments with it and swear it was the blood of

---

215. **for a true prince.** Falstaff mischievously intimates that he is glad to have this confirmation of the Prince's legitimacy. 217. **boys.** Cf. line 10. 218. **play extempore:** an improvised drama created by the actors. [s.c.] 219. **the argument:** the subject; the plot of the play. 224. **Marry.** See 1.2.18, note. 226. **a royal man.** A noble was a third of a pound sterling; a royal was half a pound. 234. **By'r Lady.** Cf. line 37. 239–240. **swear...England:** swear so many false oaths that Truth would flee the country in horror. 243. **beslubber:** daub.

true men. I did that I did not this seven year before—I blush'd to hear
his monstrous devices.   245

PRINCE.   O villain! thou stolest a cup of sack eighteen years ago and wert taken
with the manner, and ever since thou hast blush'd extempore. Thou
hadst fire and sword on thy side, and yet thou ran'st away. What
instinct hadst thou for it?

BARD.   My lord, do you see these meteors?   250
Do you behold these exhalations?

PRINCE.   I do.

BARD.   What think you they portend?

PRINCE.   Hot livers and cold purses.

BARD.   Choler, my lord, if rightly taken.   255

PRINCE.   No, if rightly taken, halter.

Enter Falstaff.

Here comes lean Jack; here comes bare-bone.
How now, my sweet creature of bombast? How long is't ago, Jack, since
thou sawest thine own knee?   259

FAL.   My own knee? When I was about thy years, Hal, I was not an eagle's
talent in the waist; I could have crept into any alderman's thumb-ring.
A plague of sighing and grief! It blows a man up like a bladder. There's
villanous news abroad. Here was Sir John Bracy from your father. You
must to the court in the morning. That same mad fellow of the North,
Percy, and he of Wales that gave Amamon the bastinado, and made
Lucifer cuckold, and swore the devil his true liegeman upon the cross
of a Welsh hook—what a plague call you him?   267

244–245. **true:** honest.—**that:** what.—Bardolph has a red nose and an inflamed countenance. See
Fluellen's description of him in *Henry V*: "His face is all bubukles and whelks, and knobs, and flames
o' fire, and his lips blows at his nose, and it is like a coal of fire, sometimes plue and sometimes red."
247. **with the manner:** in the act,—literally, with the stolen property in your possession.—**extempore.**
without premeditation. [s.c.] 250–251. **meteors…exhalations.** Synonymous. Bardolph points at his own
face with a swaggering air. 253. **portend:** threaten. Meteors were regarded as portentous phenomena. Cf.
5.1.19–21. 254. **Hot livers and cold purses:** They indicate that you have heated your liver by drinking
and emptied your purse in paying for your liquor.—**cold purses.** It is money that keeps one's purse warm.
255. **Choler,…if rightly taken:** A choleric (bilious) temperament, if properly interpreted. Bardolph's
explanation of his red face involves a warning. *Choler* meant "bile"; too much bile caused eruptions; a
bilious habit of body was accompanied by a *choleric* ("quick-tempered") disposition. 256. **No…halter.**
Prince Hal's pun is a masterpiece. In a speech only five words long he puns on three words. *Rightly, taken,*
and *halter* are all three emphasized in a voice that rises in pitch: "No, if *rightly* (justly, as you ought to
be) TAKEN (arrested)—HALTER (collar; the hangman's noose)!" 258. **creature of bombast:** stuffed
creature. *Bombast* was cotton or wool used as padding. 260–267. **talent:** talon.—**thumb-ring:** a seal ring
worn (as the fashion was) on the thumb.—**cuckold.** Falstaff alludes to Lucifer's horns. No Elizabethan
could let slip a chance to mention the horns that were said to grow on the forehead of the husband of an
unfaithful wife.—**a Welsh hook:** a kind of pike with a hook just below the point.

POINS.	O, Glendower.
FAL.	Owen, Owen—the same; and his son-in-law Mortimer, and old Northumberland, and that sprightly Scot of Scots, Douglas, that runs a-horseback up a hill perpendicular— 271
PRINCE.	He that rides at high speed and with his pistol kills a sparrow flying.
FAL.	You have hit it.
PRINCE.	So did he never the sparrow.
FAL.	Well, that rascal hath good metal in him; he will not run. 275
PRINCE.	Why, what a rascal art thou then, to praise him so for running!
FAL.	A-horseback, ye cuckoo! but afoot he will not budge a foot.
PRINCE.	Yes, Jack, upon instinct.
FAL.	I grant ye, upon instinct. Well, he is there too, and one Mordake, and a thousand bluecaps more. Worcester is stol'n away tonight; thy father's beard is turn'd white with the news; you may buy land now as cheap as stinking mack'rel. 282
PRINCE.	Why then, it is like, if there come a hot June, and this civil buffeting hold, we shall buy maidenheads as they buy hobnails, by the hundreds.
FAL.	By the mass, lad, thou sayest true; it is like we shall have good trading that way. But tell me, Hal, art not thou horrible afeard? Thou being heir apparent, could the world pick thee out three such enemies again as that fiend Douglas, that spirit Percy, and that devil Glendower? Art thou not horribly afraid? Doth not thy blood thrill at it?
PRINCE.	Not a whit, i' faith. I lack some of thy instinct. 290
FAL.	Well, thou wilt be horribly chid tomorrow when thou comest to thy father. If thou love me, practise an answer.
PRINCE.	Do thou stand for my father and examine me upon the particulars of my life.†
FAL.	Shall I? Content. This chair shall be my state, this dagger my sceptre, and this cushion my crown. 296

---

275. **metal:** material, stuff.—**run.** The pun is clear enough. Good hard metal does not *melt* easily. 277. **ye cuckoo!** Because you repeat my words without regard to their sense. 280. **bluecaps:** Scots (who wore "blue bonnets"). 281. **cheap.** Because the people fear that a revolution will result in confiscation of landed property and are eager to turn their estates into money.

---

†   In Welles's film a chair is hoisted up on one of the tavern tables and Falstaff (Welles) sits in it wearing a kitchen pot for a crown. Welles's camera shoots Falstaff (as it did the king in an earlier scene) from a low angle perspective but here the background, rather than the cold stone of Westminster, is the warm timber of the tavern's rafters. [S.C.]

Falstaff (Barry Stanton) playing the King in the "play extempore." (ESC-TV)

PRINCE.	Thy state is taken for a join'd-stool, thy golden sceptre for a leaden dagger, and thy precious rich crown for a pitiful bald crown.
FAL.	Well, an the fire of grace be not quite out of thee, now shalt thou be moved. Give me a cup of sack to make my eyes look red, that it may be thought I have wept; for I must speak in passion, and I will do it in King Cambyses' vein.
PRINCE.	Well, here is my leg.
FAL.	And here is my speech. Stand aside, nobility.
HOST.	O Jesu, this is excellent sport, i' faith! 305
FAL.	Weep not, sweet queen, for trickling tears are vain.
HOST.	O, the Father, how he holds his countenance!
FAL.	For God's sake, lords, convey my tristful queen! For tears do stop the floodgates of her eyes.
HOST.	O Jesu, he doth it as like one of these harlotry players as ever I see! 310

301–302. **passion:** strong emotion.—**King Cambyses' vein:** i.e., style. Thomas Preston's ridiculous tragedy *Cambyses, King of Persia* was printed about 1570. Shakespeare doubtless had it in mind, though Preston's idea of an emotional style is very different from Falstaff's. 303. **my leg:** an elaborate bow—one leg being drawn back and the other knee bent. 308. **convey:** escort her hence.—**tristful:** sorrowful. 310. **these harlotry players:** these rascals of players. The Hostess uses the word lightly—not in condemnation. Compare the use of *rogue, rascal,* etc., as pet names for children.

Hal (Michael Pennington) playing the King in the "play extempore." (ESC-TV)

FAL. Peace, good pintpot. Peace, good tickle-brain.—Harry, I do not
only marvel where thou spendest thy time, but also how thou art
accompanied. For though the camomile, the more it is trodden on, the
faster it grows, yet youth, the more it is wasted, the sooner it wears.
That thou art my son I have partly thy mother's word, partly my
own opinion, but chiefly a villanous trick of thine eye and a foolish
hanging of thy nether lip that doth warrant me. If then thou be son to
me, here lies the point: why, being son to me, art thou so pointed at?
Shall the blessed sun of heaven prove a micher and eat blackberries?
A question not to be ask'd. Shall the son of England prove a thief and
take purses? A question to be ask'd. There is a thing, Harry, which thou
hast often heard of, and it is known to many in our land by the name
of pitch. This pitch, as ancient writers do report, doth defile; so doth
the company thou keepest. For, Harry, now I do not speak to thee in

---

311. **Peace.** Falstaff is forced to drop his play-acting for a moment, since his histrionic speeches in lines
306–308 have served only to prompt Dame Quickly to admiring interruption. He calls the Hostess by
names suggested by her occupation.—**tickle-brain.** A cant word for strong drink. 313. **the camomile.**
Falstaff is imitating the style of Lyly's *Euphues*. We are not to infer, however (as some critics do), that
Shakespeare means to ridicule or satirize Lyly, who was one of England's leading playwrights when
Shakespeare began his dramatic career. [s.c.] Parody is not necessarily ridicule, and Shakespeare often
shows the influence of *Euphues* in serious passages. 314. **micher:** a truant; a boy who, instead of going to
school, sneaks off into a blackberry patch. 323. **pitch...defile.** "He that toucheth pitch shall be defiled"
(*Ecclesiasticus*, xiii, 1).

drink, but in tears; not in pleasure, but in passion; not in words only, but in woes also: and yet there is a virtuous man whom I have often noted in thy company, but I know not his name.   327

PRINCE.   What manner of man, an it like your Majesty?

FAL.   A goodly portly man, i' faith, and a corpulent; of a cheerful look, a pleasing eye, and a most noble carriage; and, as I think, his age some fifty, or, by'r Lady, inclining to threescore; and now I remember me, his name is Falstaff. If that man should be lewdly given, he deceiveth me; for, Harry, I see virtue in his looks. If then the tree may be known by the fruit, as the fruit by the tree, then, peremptorily I speak it, there is virtue in that Falstaff. Him keep with, the rest banish. And tell me now, thou naughty varlet, tell me where hast thou been this month?

PRINCE.   Dost thou speak like a king? Do thou stand for me, and I'll play my father.   338

FAL.   Depose me? If thou dost it half so gravely, so majestically, both in word and matter, hang me up by the heels for a rabbit-sucker or a poulter's hare.

PRINCE.   Well, here I am set.

FAL.   And here I stand. Judge, my masters.

PRINCE.   Now, Harry, whence come you?

FAL.   My noble lord, from Eastcheap.   345

PRINCE.   The complaints I hear of thee are grievous.

FAL.   'Sblood, my lord, they are false! Nay, I'll tickle ye for a young prince, i' faith.

PRINCE.   Swearest thou, ungracious boy? Henceforth ne'er look on me. Thou art violently carried away from grace. There is a devil haunts thee in the likeness of an old fat man; a tun of man is thy companion. Why dost thou converse with that trunk of humours, that bolting hutch of beastliness, that swoll'n parcel of dropsies, that huge bombard of sack,

---

325. **passion:** bitter grief. 329. **goodly:** handsome.—**portly:** stately; of imposing appearance. —**corpulent:** full-bodied—not in the modern sense of "extremely stout." 332. **lewdly given:** inclined to low conduct. *Lewd* was a general term for "base," "disreputable." 312–314. **the tree...by the fruit.** "The tree is known by his fruit" (*Matthew*, xii, 33).—**peremptorily:** positively; without fear of contradiction. 336. **naughty varlet:** bad boy. Falstaff suddenly drops the elaborate preaching style and speaks like an ordinary father scolding a youngster who has misbehaved. 337. **Dost thou speak like a king?** Prince Hal refers especially to Falstaff's last sentence. 340. **a rabbit-sucker:** a sucking rabbit (not yet weaned).—**a poulter's hare:** i.e., one hung up (for sale) at the door of a poulterer's (poultry dealer's) shop. 347. **'Sblood.** See 1.2.56, note. —**I'll tickle ye for a young prince:** I'll play the young prince in a style that shall make you jump! 349–50. **ungracious:** graceless.—**grace:** virtue. 352–353. **converse:** associate.— **humours:** morbid secretions in the body; practically equivalent to "diseases."—**bolting hutch:** huge receptacle—literally, a bin into which flour falls when it is sifted. —**bombard:** a leather wine vessel.

Hal (Keith Baxter) playing his father and Falstaff (Orson Welles) playing Hal. (Welles's *Chimes at Midnight*)

	that stuff'd cloakbag of guts, that roasted Manningtree ox with the pudding in his belly, that reverend vice, that grey iniquity, that father ruffian, that vanity in years? Wherein is he good, but to taste sack and drink it? wherein neat and cleanly, but to carve a capon and eat it? wherein cunning, but in craft? wherein crafty, but in villany? wherein villanous, but in all things? wherein worthy, but in nothing? 359
FAL.	I would your Grace would take me with you. Whom means your Grace?
PRINCE.	That villanous abominable misleader of youth, Falstaff, that old white-bearded Satan.
FAL.	My lord, the man I know.
PRINCE.	I know thou dost. 365
FAL.	But to say I know more harm in him than in myself were to say more than I know. That he is old (the more the pity) his white hairs do witness it; but that he is (saving your reverence) a whoremaster, that I

354–358. **Manningtree ox.** Manningtree in Essex appears to have been celebrated for fat cattle and barbecues as well as for morality plays acted by local talent. —**pudding:** sausage.—**vice:** the comic character in the old morality plays—impersonating Iniquity in general or some particular sin. —**that vanity in years:** that aged impersonation of folly and worldliness. —**cunning:** skilful. 360. **your Grace:** your Majesty. Not, in Shakespeare's time, limited to the title of a duke.—**take me with you:** Slow down so I can follow what you are saying. [s.c.] 368. **saving your reverence.** An apologetic phrase spoken with no intention of offending and was used (often by persons of inferior rank) in mentioning something indecent or unpleasant.

utterly deny. If sack and sugar be a fault, God help the wicked! If to be old and merry be a sin, then many an old host that I know is damn'd. If to be fat be to be hated, then Pharaoh's lean kine are to be loved. No, my good lord. Banish Peto, banish Bardolph, banish Poins; but for sweet Jack Falstaff, kind Jack Falstaff, true Jack Falstaff, valiant Jack Falstaff, and therefore more valiant being, as he is, old Jack Falstaff, banish not him thy Harry's company, banish not him thy Harry's company. Banish plump Jack, and banish all the world!   376

PRINCE.   I do, I will.‡   [*A knocking heard.*]
                                   [*Exeunt Hostess, Francis, and Bardolph.*]

                        Enter Bardolph, *running.*

BARD.   O, my lord, my lord! the sheriff with a most monstrous watch is at the door.

FAL.   Out, ye rogue! Play out the play. I have much to say in the behalf of that Falstaff.   381

                          Enter the Hostess.

HOST.   O Jesu, my lord, my lord!

PRINCE.   Heigh, heigh, the devil rides upon a fiddlestick! What's the matter?

HOST.   The sheriff and all the watch are at the door. They are come to search the house. Shall I let them in?   385

FAL.   Dost thou hear, Hal? Never call a true piece of gold a counterfeit. Thou art essentially mad without seeming so.

PRINCE.   And thou a natural coward without instinct.

FAL.   I deny your major. If you will deny the sheriff, so; if not, let him enter. If I become not a cart as well as another man, a plague on my bringing up! I hope I shall as soon be strangled with a halter as another.   391

---

371. **Pharaoh's lean kine.** See *Genesis,* xli, 18–21. 377. **I do, I will:** Hal's implied threat cannot be given time to be absorbed by Falstaff which is why Shakespeare interrupts the moment with the monstrous watch come knocking at the door. [S.C.] 380. **Out:** Come, come! A protesting interjection. 383. **the devil rides upon a fiddlestick!** The Prince refers to the hostess's excitement: "You have something marvellous to report! What's all this hubbub about?" 386. **Never call...a counterfeit.** One cannot be absolutely certain what Falstaff means. Either of two interpretations makes good sense: (1) "Believe what the hostess is telling you"; (2) "Take me for what I am—genuine gold, and no sham." The former fits the situation and the context better. 389–390. **I deny your major.** A stock phrase in a formal argument: "I deny your major premise." *Major* was almost or quite identical in pronunciation with *mayor.* Hence Falstaff's pun.—**deny the sheriff:** refuse to admit him.—**so:** well and good.—**a cart:** in which criminals are carried to the gallows.

---

‡   How does the actor deliver these lines (with a laugh? with a wicked smile? with a stern command?) and how does the actor playing Falstaff (playing the prince) respond? How long does the director allow Hal's promise and threat to hang in the air before the sheriff's knocking begins at the door? [S.C.]

PRINCE.   Go hide thee behind the arras. The rest walk up above. Now, my masters, for a true face and good conscience.

FAL.   Both which I have had; but their date is out, and therefore I'll hide me.

                                                                    Exit.

PRINCE.   Call in the sheriff.   395

                          [*Exeunt. Manent the Prince and Peto.*]

                  Enter Sheriff *and the* Carrier.

          Now, Master Sheriff, what is your will with me?

SHER.   First, pardon me, my lord. A hue and cry
          Hath followed certain men unto this house.

PRINCE.   What men?

SHER.   One of them is well known, my gracious lord—   400
          A gross fat man.

CARRIER.   As fat as butter.

PRINCE.   The man, I do assure you, is not here,
          For I myself at this time have employ'd him.
          And, sheriff, I will engage my word to thee
          That I will by tomorrow dinner time   405
          Send him to answer thee, or any man,
          For anything he shall be charg'd withal;
          And so let me entreat you leave the house.

SHER.   I will, my lord. There are two gentlemen
          Have in this robbery lost three hundred marks   410

PRINCE.   It may be so. If he have robb'd these men,
          He shall be answerable; and so farewell.

SHER.   Good night, my noble lord.

PRINCE.   I think it is good morrow, is it not?

SHER.   Indeed, my lord, I think it be two o'clock.   *Exit* [*with Carrier*]. 415

PRINCE.   This oily rascal is known as well as
          Paul's. Go call him forth.

PETO.   Falstaff! Fast asleep behind the arras, and snorting like a horse.

392–393. **the arras.** The tapestry hangings were supported on frames at some distance from the walls.—**true:** honest. S.d.: **Manent:** remain (Latin). [S.C.] 397. **A hue and cry:** a general muster of citizens in pursuit of a criminal. 402. **not here.** Prince Hal makes what used to be called a "mental reservation":—"not *here*, but behind the arras." Thus he equivocates, avoiding a direct lie. A gesture, no doubt, served to emphasize *here*. 404. **engage:** pledge. 407. **withal:** with. Often so used at the end of a clause. 414. **morrow:** morning. 417. **Paul's:** Saint Paul's Church in London. 418. **Fast asleep.** Falstaff relies upon the Prince to see him safely through this affair; but even so, his nonchalance is proof enough that he has little fear of the consequences. [S.C.]

PRINCE.   Hark how hard he fetches breath.
           Search his pockets.   420

                    He searcheth his pockets and findeth certain papers.

           What hast thou found?

PETO.   Nothing but papers, my lord.

PRINCE.   Let's see what they be. Read them.

PETO.   [*reads*] 'Item, A capon…2 s. 2 d.
           Item, Sauce…4 d.   425
           Item, Sack two gallons 5 s. 8 d.
           Item, Anchovies and
           Sack after supper…2 s. 6 d.
           Item, Bread…ob.'   429

PRINCE.   O monstrous! but one halfpennyworth of bread to this intolerable deal
           of sack! What there is else, keep close; we'll read it at more advantage.
           There let him sleep till day. I'll to the court in the morning. We must
           all to the wars, and thy place shall be honourable. I'll procure this fat
           rogue a charge of foot; and I know his death will be a march of twelve
           score. The money shall be paid back again with advantage. Be with me
           betimes in the morning, and so good morrow, Peto.   436

PETO.   Good morrow, good my lord.   *Exeunt.*

ACT III

SCENE I. [*Bangor, Wales. Glendower's house.*]

Enter Hotspur, Worcester, Lord Mortimer, Owen Glendower.

MORT.   These promises are fair, the parties sure,
           And our induction full of prosperous hope.

HOT.   Lord Mortimer, and cousin Glendower,
           Will you sit down?

---

426. **s. (shilling) and d. (pence):** English units of monetary measure. [s.c.] 429. **ob.** An abbreviation
for *obolus* (a small Greek coin)—"halfpenny." 431–436. **close:** secret.—**at more advantage:** when we
have a better opportunity.—**a charge of foot:** a company of infantry.—**twelve score:** i.e., yards. The
Prince adopts the method of measuring used in archery. The English war arrow was a cloth-yard in
length.—**with advantage:** with addition.—**betimes:** in good season; early.
ACT III. SCENE I.
Holinshed sets this meeting at the house of the Archdeacon of Bangor in Wales but Shakespeare appears to
set the scene at Glendower's home, also in Wales. 2. **induction.** An *induction* is an introductory scene which
precedes the first act of a play. See *The Taming of the Shrew.*—**prosperous hope:** hope of prospering.

| | And uncle Worcester. A plague upon it! | 5 |
| | I have forgot the map. | |

GLEND.   No, here it is.
Sit, cousin Percy; sit, good cousin Hotspur,
For by that name as oft as Lancaster
Doth speak of you, his cheek looks pale, and with
A rising sigh he wisheth you in heaven.   10

HOT.   And you in hell, as oft as he hears
Owen Glendower spoke of.

GLEND.   I cannot blame him. At my nativity
The front of heaven was full of fiery shapes
Of burning cressets, and at my birth   15
The frame and huge foundation of the earth
Shak'd like a coward.

HOT.   Why, so it would have done at the same season, if your mother's cat
had but kitten'd, though yourself had never been born.

GLEND.   I say the earth did shake when I was born.   20

HOT.   And I say the earth was not of my mind,
If you suppose as fearing you it shook.

GLEND.   The heavens were all on fire, the earth did tremble.

HOT.   O, then the earth shook to see the heavens on fire,
And not in fear of your nativity.   25
Diseased nature oftentimes breaks forth
In strange eruptions; oft the teeming earth
Is with a kind of colic pinch'd and vex'd
By the imprisoning of unruly wind
Within her womb, which, for enlargement striving,   30
Shakes the old beldame earth and topples down
Steeples and mossgrown towers. At your birth
Our grandam earth, having this distemp'rature,
In passion shook.

GLEND.   Cousin, of many men
I do not bear these crossings. Give me leave   35
To tell you once again that at my birth
The front of heaven was full of fiery shapes,

13–15. **nativity:** birth.—**front:** literally, forehead (Latin *frons*).—**cressets:** a kind of torch, consisting of a small metal fire-basket filled with combustibles and attached to the end of a pole so as to swing on a pivot. 27–34. Hotspur expounds, in figurative language, the scientific theory which had come down from classical times and which was currently accepted in Shakespeare's day. 30–34. **enlargement:** release from imprisonment [s.c.].—**beldame:** old lady—**distemp'rature:** disorder, ailment.—**passion:** suffering.—**crossings:** thwarting, interruptions. [s.c.]—**of:** from.

The goats ran from the mountains, and the herds
Were strangely clamorous to the frighted fields,
These signs have mark'd me extraordinary,   40
And all the courses of my life do show
I am not in the roll of common men.
Where is he living, clipp'd in with the sea
That chides the banks of England, Scotland, Wales,
Which calls me pupil or hath read to me?   45
And bring him out that is but woman's son
Can trace me in the tedious ways of art
And hold me pace in deep experiments.

HOT.   I think there's no man speaks better
Welsh. I'll to dinner.   50

MORT.   Peace, cousin Percy; you will make him mad.

GLEND.   I can call spirits from the vasty deep.

HOT.   Why, so can I, or so can any man;
But will they come when you do call for them?[†]

GLEND.   Why, I can teach you, cousin, to command   55
The devil.

HOT.   And I can teach thee, coz, to shame the devil—
By telling truth. Tell truth and shame the devil.
If thou have power to raise him, bring him hither,
And I'll be sworn I have power to shame him hence.   60
O, while you live, tell truth and shame the devil!

MORT.   Come, come, no more of this unprofitable chat.

GLEND.   Three times hath Henry Bolingbroke made head
Against my power; thrice from the banks of Wye
And sandy-bottom'd Severn have I sent him   65
Bootless home and weather-beaten back.

HOT.   Home without boots, and in foul weather too?
How scapes he agues, in the devil's name?

44–48. **clipp'd in with:** enclosed by; within the limits of.—**read to me:** given me instruction.—**trace:** follow.—**art:** art magic.—**hold me pace:** keep up with me.—**deep:** occult. 50. **Welsh.** Hotspur suggests that ability to speak Welsh is a magical accomplishment. 52. **the vasty deep:** the lower world. [s.c.] 57. **coz:** cousin. 58. **Tell truth and shame the devil.** An old proverb. Truth shames the devil because he is "the father of lies." 63. **made head:** mustered an army. *Head* for "an armed force" is common. 66. **Bootless:** unsuccessful—literally, without advantage.—**weather-beaten:** i.e., by storms raised by my magic.

---

† Hotspur's humor is wickedly funny here but he is provoking an important ally; one who, eventually, does not come to Hotspur's support at Shrewsbury. Does the actor playing Hotspur show any flicker of recognition that his wit comes at the expense of diplomacy here? [s.c.]

GLEND.	Come, here's the map. Shall we divide our right	
	According to our threefold order ta'en?	70
MORT.	The Archdeacon hath divided it	
	Into three limits very equally.	
	England, from Trent and Severn hitherto,	
	By south and east is to my part assign'd;	
	All westward, Wales beyond the Severn shore,	75
	And all the fertile land within that bound,	
	To Owen Glendower; and, dear coz, to you	
	The remnant northward lying off from Trent.	
	And our indentures tripartite are drawn;	
	Which being sealed interchangeably	80
	(A business that this night may execute),	
	Tomorrow, cousin Percy, you and I	
	And my good Lord of Worcester will set forth	
	To meet your father and the Scottish power,	
	As is appointed us, at Shrewsbury.	85
	My father Glendower is not ready yet,	
	Nor shall we need his help these fourteen days.	
	[*To Glend.*] Within that space you may have drawn together	
	Your tenants, friends, and neighbouring gentlemen.	
GLEND.	A shorter time shall send me to you, lords;	90
	And in my conduct shall your ladies come,	
	From whom you now must steal and take no leave,	
	For there will be a world of water shed	
	Upon the parting of your wives and you.	
HOT.	Methinks my moiety, north from Burton here,	95
	In quantity equals not one of yours.	
	See how this river comes me cranking in	
	And cuts me from the best of all my land	
	A huge half-moon, a monstrous cantle out.	
	I'll have the current in this place damm'd up,	100
	And here the smug and silver Trent shall run	
	In a new channel fair and evenly.	
	It shall not wind with such a deep indent	

rebellion starting to dissolve

69–77. **our right:** the territory that rightfully belongs to us.—**our threefold order ta'en:** the arrangement we have made for a division into three parts. 72. **limits:** well defined districts. 73. **hitherto:** up to this line. He points at the map. 79–81. **indentures tripartite:** contracts to which all three of us are parties.—**drawn:** drawn up.—**may:** can. 84. **father:** father-in-law. 88. **may have:** will be able to have. 91. **in my conduct:** escorted by me. 95. **moiety:** share. The word was not confined, as in modern English, to "half." 97–102. **cranking:** winding; with a turn in its course.—**cantle:** section, segment.—**smug:** smooth. Often used in the sense of "trimly dressed," "spruce." Hotspur is playing with the word.—**fair and evenly:** in a direct course. One *-ly* serves for two adverbs.

	To rob me of so rich a bottom here.	
GLEND.	Not wind? It shall, it must! You see it doth.	105
MORT.	Yea, but	
	Mark how he bears his course, and runs me up	
	With like advantage on the other side,	
	Gelding the opposed continent as much	
	As on the other side it takes from you.	110
WOR.	Yea, but a little charge will trench him here	
	And on this north side win this cape of land;	
	And then he runs straight and even.	
HOT.	I'll have it so. A little charge will do it.	
GLEND.	I will not have it alt'red.	
HOT.	Will not you?	115
GLEND.	No, nor you shall not.	
HOT.	Who shall say me nay?	
GLEND.	Why, that will I.	
HOT.	Let me not understand you then; speak it in Welsh.	
GLEND.	I can speak English, lord, as well as you;	
	For I was train'd up in the English court,	120
	Where, being but young, I framed to the harp	
	Many an English ditty lovely well,	
	And gave the tongue a helpful ornament—	
	A virtue that was never seen in you.	
HOT.	Marry,	125
	And I am glad of it with all my heart!	
	I had rather be a kitten and cry mew	
	Than one of these same metre ballad-mongers.	
	I had rather hear a brazen canstick turn'd	
	Or a dry wheel grate on the axletree,	130
	And that would set my teeth nothing on edge,	

---

104. **bottom:** a tract of low alluvial land. 109. **Gelding...as much:** cutting out as large a piece from the opposite bank. A *continent* is, literally, a "container," "that which holds something in." 114. **charge:** expense. 120. **in the English court.** Holinshed records that Glendower, in his youth, was "set to studie the lawes of the realme, and became an vtter barrester, or an apprentise of the law,...and serued king Richard at Flint castell." 122–124. **I framed to the harp...ditty:** I composed many songs in English for tunes played on the harp. *Ditty* (from Old French *dité, ditié*) is the regular term for the "words" of a song.—**a helpful ornament.** Glendower means that his songs not only adorned the English language but also helped to develop it for elegant literary use. 124. **a virtue:** an accomplishment. 128. **ballet-mongers:** dealers in ballads, poetasters, rhymers. Used for "poets" in humorous contempt. 129. **canstick:** candlestick.—**turn'd:** i.e., on a lathe.

	Nothing so much as mincing poetry.	
	'Tis like the forc'd gait of a shuffling nag.	
GLEND.	Come, you shall have Trent turn'd.	
HOT.	I do not care. I'll give thrice so much land	135
	To any well-deserving friend;	
	But in the way of bargain, mark ye me,	
	I'll cavil on the ninth part of a hair.	
	Are the indentures drawn? Shall we be gone?	
GLEND.	The moon shines fair; you may away by night.	140
	I'll haste the writer, and withal	
	Break with your wives of your departure hence.	
	I am afraid my daughter will run mad,	
	So much she doteth on her Mortimer.	*Exit*
MORT.	Fie, cousin Percy! how you cross my father!	145
HOT.	I cannot choose. Sometime he angers me	
	With telling me of the moldwarp and the ant,	
	Of the dreamer Merlin and his prophecies,	
	And of a dragon and a finless fish,	
	A clip-wing'd griffin and a moulten raven,	150
	A couching lion and a ramping cat,	
	And such a deal of skimble-skamble stuff	
	As puts me from my faith. I tell you what—	
	He held me last night at least nine hours	
	In reckoning up the several devils' names	155
	That were his lackeys. I cried "hum," and "Well, go to!"	
	But mark'd him not a word. O, he is as tedious	
	As a tired horse, a railing wife;	
	Worse than a smoky house. I had rather live	

132. **mincing:** walking with short and carefully measured steps. 133. **the forc'd gait of a shuffling nag:** the mincing steps of a tricky horse whose legs have been confined in order to force him to take a regular gait. 141–142. **withal:** also, likewise.—**Break with:** broach the subject to; inform.—**of:** concerning. 145. **cross:** vex (by contradiction, etc.). 146. **I cannot choose:** I cannot help it. 149–153. Holinshed writes that the division just discussed was made "(as some haue said) through a foolish credit given to a vaine prophesie, as though king Henrie was *the moldwarpe*, cursed of Gods owne mouth, and they three were the *dragon,* the *lion,* and the woolfe, which should diuide this realme betweene them." 147. **moldwarp:** mole—so called because it *warps* (throws up) the mold (the soil). 148–150. **Merlin.** The famous prophet of the Arthurian legend. —**a moulten raven:** a raven that had moulted— cast off most of its feathers. 151–153. **couching...ramping:** couchant ("lying down," "crouching"); rampant ("standing on its hind legs and pawing the air")—heraldic terms.—**skimble-skamble stuff:** nonsensical rigmarole.—**puts me from my faith:** makes me so incredulous that I can no longer believe even my creed as a Christian. 156. **go to!** literally, "go away!" used like our "go way" (which is an old idiom) to express surprise or incredulity or as mere interjection of protest. Hotspur means, not that he scoffed at Glendower's story, but that he paid only so much attention as enabled him to pretend polite astonishment. 158–159. **a railing wife...a smoky house.** Compare with the proverb "a smoking house and a railing wife make a man run out of doors."

	With cheese and garlic in a windmill far	160
	Than feed on cates and have him talk to me	
	In any summer house in Christendom.	
MORT.	In faith, he is a worthy gentleman,	
	Exceedingly well read, and profited	
	In strange concealments, valiant as a lion,	165
	And wondrous affable, and as bountiful	
	As mines of India. Shall I tell you, cousin?	
	He holds your temper in a high respect	
	And curbs himself even of his natural scope	
	When you come 'cross his humor. Faith, he does.	170
	I warrant you that man is not alive	
	Might so have tempted him as you have done	
	Without the taste of danger and reproof.	
	But do not use it oft, let me entreat you.	
WOR.	In faith, my lord, you are too wilful-blame,	175
	And since your coming hither have done enough	
	To put him quite besides his patience.	
	You must needs learn, lord, to amend this fault.	
	Though sometimes it show greatness, courage, blood—	
	And that's the dearest grace it renders you—	180
	Yet oftentimes it doth present harsh rage,	
	Defect of manners, want of government,	
	Pride, haughtiness, opinion, and disdain;	
	The least of which haunting a nobleman	
	Loseth men's hearts, and leaves behind a stain	185
	Upon the beauty of all parts besides,	
	Beguiling them of commendation.	
HOT.	Well, I am school'd. Good manners be your speed!	
	Here come our wives, and let us take our leave.	

Enter Glendower *with the* Ladies.

161–162. **cates:** delicate food.—**summer house:** a rich man's "summer residence." 163. **worthy:** honourable. 164–165. **profited...concealments:** proficient in wonderful secrets (of magic). 168–170. **He holds...respect:** he is very considerate of your hasty temperament.—**scope:** freedom of speech.— **come 'cross his humor:** say something that tends to put him out of humor.—**Faith:** in faith; upon my word. 172–173. **Might:** could.—**tempted:** provoked.—**Without the taste...reproof:** without having experienced some rebuke that would have been dangerous to you. 174. **use it:** practise it. 175–177. **too wilful-blame:** too blameworthy for your wilfulness—for insisting on having your own way.—**besides his patience:** beyond the bounds of self-control. 179–187. **blood:** high spirit.—**the dearest grace...you:** the most notable honor it does you.—**present:** show.—**government:** self-control.—**opinion:** self-opinion, self-conceit.—**of which:** of which faults.—**Loseth:** causes the loss of; makes him lose.—**parts:** good qualities.—**Beguiling them of commendation:** causing them to lose (cheating them out of) the praise that they deserve. 188. **I am school'd:** I have had my lesson.—**be your speed:** give you good fortune; cause you to prosper.

MORT.	This is the deadly spite that angers me—	190
	My wife can speak no English, I no Welsh.	
GLEND.	My daughter weeps; she will not part with you;†	
	She'll be a soldier too, she'll to the wars.	
MORT.	Good father, tell her that she and my aunt Percy	
	Shall follow in your conduct speedily.	195

Glendower speaks to her in Welsh, and she answers him in the same.

GLEND.	She is desperate here. A peevish self-will'd harlotry,	
	One that no persuasion can do good upon.	

The Lady speaks in Welsh.

MORT.	I understand thy looks. That pretty Welsh	
	Which thou pourest down from these swelling heavens	
	I am too perfect in; and, but for shame,	200
	In such a parley should I answer thee.	

The Lady again in Welsh.

I understand thy kisses, and thou mine,
And that's a feeling disputation.
But I will never be a truant, love,
Till I have learnt thy language; for thy tongue   205
Makes Welsh as sweet as ditties highly penn'd,
Sung by a fair queen in a summer's bow'r,
With ravishing division, to her lute.

GLEND.	Nay, if you melt, then will she run mad.	

The Lady speaks again in Welsh.

MORT.	O, I am ignorance itself in this!	210
GLEND.	She bids you on the wanton rushes lay you down	

---

190. **spite:** vexation; vexatious circumstance. 194–195. **aunt.** Lady Percy was Sir Edmund Mortimer's sister. She was aunt to Edmund Mortimer, Earl of March.—**in your conduct:** under your escort. 196. Glendower explains what the lady has said. She has insisted on accompanying her husband.—**desperate here:** a hopeless case—beyond the possibility of persuasion on *this* point.—**peevish:** childish.—**harlotry:** jade. Used, like *wench,* as a fancifully affectionate word. *Rogue, rascal, wretch, fool,* etc., are similarly used. 198–201. **That pretty Welsh:** your tears.—**perfect in:** well versed in.—**In such a parley:** in the same kind of discourse. 203. **a feeling disputation:** a heartfelt discussion—exchange of sentiments. 206. **ditties.** See line 122, note. 209. **division:** modulation, harmony. 211. **the wanton rushes:** the rushes which covered the floor of the house (and the stage) instead of a carpet or rug. *Wanton* means, literally, "unrestrained" and is used in a great variety of special senses. Here it suggests comfort and luxurious ease: "this soft carpet of plentiful rushes."

---

† This section of the scene set at Glendower's castle in Wales is often cut, but is important because it reintroduces the female voice and perspective on war. The difficulty of communicating between the genders is underlined by the fact that Mortimer speaks no Welsh; his wife no English. The beauty of the Welsh language and Lady Mortimer's singing stands in contrast to the harsh language of military conflict which follows. The scene is presented in full in the ESC version, perhaps because the director, Michael Bogdanov, is part Welsh. [s.c.]

And rest your gentle head upon her lap,
And she will sing the song that pleaseth you
And on your eyelids crown the god of sleep,
Charming your blood with pleasing heaviness,   215
Making such difference 'twixt wake and sleep
As is the difference betwixt day and night
The hour before the heavenly-harness'd team
Begins his golden progress in the East.

MORT.   With all my heart I'll sit and hear her sing.   220
          By that time will our book, I think, be drawn.

GLEND.   Do so,
          And those musicians that shall play to you
          Hang in the air a thousand leagues from hence,
          And straight they shall be here. Sit, and attend.

HOT.   Come, Kate, thou art perfect in lying down. Come, quick, quick, that
          I may lay my head in thy lap.   226

LADY.   Go, ye giddy goose.   *The music plays.*

HOT.   Now I perceive the devil understands Welsh;
          And 'tis no marvel, he is so humorous.
          By'r Lady, he is a good musician.   230

LADY P.   Then should you be nothing but musical; for you are altogether
          govern'd by humours. Lie still, ye thief, and hear the lady sing in
          Welsh.

HOT.   I had rather hear Lady, my brach, howl in Irish.

LADY P.   Wouldst thou have thy head broken?   235

HOT.   No.

LADY P.   Then be still.

HOT.   Neither! 'Tis a woman's fault.

LADY P.   Now God help thee!

---

214. **crown the god of sleep:** give sleep its sway. 215–209. **heaviness:** drowsiness.—**such difference...**
East: partaking of sleep and wakefulness, as the twilight of night and day. 221. **our book:** the
"indentures" mentioned in lines 79, 139.—**drawn:** finished in a fair copy and ready to be sealed. 222.
those musicians...here. Glendower promises to summon spirits of the air to play the music. 229–230.
'tis no marvel, he is so humorous: after all, it is no wonder that the devil understands Welsh: he is so
whimsical a fellow that he might naturally take a fancy to learn such a strange language.—**By'r Lady.**
See 2.4.37, note. 232. **humours:** whims, notions. 234. **brach:** a bitch hound. —**in Irish.** We may infer
that Hotspur's hound was of Irish breed; or perhaps he is thinking of wolves, which were not extinct in
Ireland until long after Shakespeare's time. 235. **head broken.** Lady Percy makes a threatening gesture
with her fan. 238. **Neither!...fault:** No, I won't be still either! To hold one's tongue is a *woman's* fault,
and I am a man. Hotspur jestingly reverses a time-honoured proposition. He had often been accused of
being as talkative as a woman. 239. **God help thee!** for *I* give thee up.

Hot.	To the Welsh lady's bed.	240
Lady P.	What's that?	
Hot.	Peace! she sings.	

Here the Lady sings a Welsh song.

Come, Kate, I'll have your song too.

Lady P.	Not mine, in good sooth.

Hot.   Not yours, in good sooth? Heart! you swear like a comfit-maker's wife.
"Not you, in good sooth!" and "as true as I live!" and "as God shall
mend me!" and "as sure as day!"   247
And givest such sarcenet surety for thy oaths
As if thou ne'er walk'st further than Finsbury.
Swear me, Kate, like a lady as thou art,   250
A good mouth-filling oath; and leave "in sooth"
And such protest of pepper gingerbread
To velvet guards and Sunday citizens.
Come, sing.

Lady P.   I will not sing.   255

Hot.   'Tis the next way to turn tailor or be redbreast-teacher. An the
indentures be drawn, I'll away within these two hours; and so come in
when ye will.   *Exit.*

Glend.   Come, come, Lord Mortimer. You are as slow
As hot Lord Percy is on fire to go.   260
By this our book is drawn; we'll but seal,
And then to horse immediately.

Mort.   With all my heart.   *Exeunt.*

---

244. **sooth:** truth. 245. **Heart!** A clipped form of the oath "by God's heart."—**comfit-maker's:** confectioner's. 246. **mend:** amend. 248. **sarcenet:** slight, trivial. *Sarcenet* is a kind of thin silk, used especially for linings. It does not give much strength to the garment it lines. 249. **As if...Finsbury:** as if you were the wife of a citizen of London. Finsbury was in Shakespeare's day a recreation ground outside of the city—a favourite resort for Londoners on Sundays and holidays. 252–253. **protést:** affirmation—not strong enough to be called an oath.—**of pepper gingerbread:** of no more firmness or solidity than a crumbly substance like gingerbread.—**guards:** trimmings, such as adorned citizens' best attire. 256. **'Tis the next way:** Well, if you won't sing, don't! Perhaps you're right in refusing. After all, singing is the nearest way to becoming a tailor or a bird-teacher—and nobody wishes you to take up either of those trades. 261. **By this:** by this time. See line 221, note.

SCENE II. [*London. The Palace.*]

Enter the King, Prince of Wales, *and others.*

KING.   Lords, give us leave. The Prince of Wales and I†
            Must have some private conference; but be near at hand,
            For we shall presently have need of you.   *Exeunt Lords.*
            I know not whether God will have it so,
            For some displeasing service I have done,   5
            That, in his secret doom, out of my blood
            He'll breed revengement and a scourge for me;
            But thou dost in thy passages of life
            Make me believe that thou art only mark'd
            For the hot vengeance and the rod of heaven   10
            To punish my mistreadings. Tell me else,
            Could such inordinate and low desires,
            Such poor, such bare, such lewd, such mean attempts,
            Such barren pleasures, rude society,
            As thou art match'd withal and grafted to,   15
            Accompany the greatness of thy blood
            And hold their level with thy princely heart?

PRINCE.   So please your Majesty, I would I could
            Quit all offences with as clear excuse
            As well as I am doubtless I can purge   20
            Myself of many I am charg'd withal.
            Yet such extenuation let me beg
            As, in reproof of many tales devis'd,

Scene II.
The scene is set in the king's chambers at Westminster. 1. **give us leave:** allow us to be alone. A regular form of polite dismissal. 5. **some displeasing service…done:** some lapse from duty in serving him. 6, 7. **doom:** judgment, decree.—**out…for me:** he means to bring vengeance and punishment upon me that shall be the direct outcome of my own son's acts. 8. **thy passages of life:** the actions of thy life. 11. **my.** Emphatic.—**mistreadings:** false steps; transgressions.—**else:** if that were not the case. 12. **inordinate:** irregular (not suitable to thy order, thy "rank")—not, excessive. 13. **lewd:** vulgar, low.—**attempts:** undertakings, exploits. 15–17. **withal:** with.—**grafted to:** as a graft becomes an integral part of the tree to which it is grafted.—**hold their level with:** satisfy. 19–21. **Quit:** acquit myself of; prove my innocence of.—**all…many.** Both emphatic.—**doubtless:** certain, confident.—**purge.** Synonymous with *quit.* 22, 23. **such extenuation:** such a degree of moderation in the judgment passed upon me.— **in reproof of:** when I shall disprove.—**tales devis'd:** made-up stories; fictitious tales.

---

†   In the BBC production, Jon Finch, who played the king, was carefully washing his hands as the scene begins, revealing that beneath the king's anger and disappointment with his son resides his own tainted conscience for his overthrow and eventual murder of Richard II. [s.c.]

Which oft the ear of greatness needs must hear
By smiling pickthanks and base newsmongers,   25
I may, for some things true wherein my youth
Hath faulty wand'red and irregular,
Find pardon on my true submission.

KING.   God pardon thee! Yet let me wonder, Harry,
At thy affections, which do hold a wing   30
Quite from the flight of all thy ancestors.
Thy place in Council thou hast rudely lost,
Which by thy younger brother is supplied,
And art almost an alien to the hearts
Of all the court and princes of my blood.   35
The hope and expectation of thy time
Is ruin'd, and the soul of every man
Prophetically do forethink thy fall.
Had I so lavish of my presence been,
So common-hackney'd in the eyes of men,   40
So stale and cheap to vulgar company,
Opinion, that did help me to the crown,
Had still kept loyal to possession
And left me in reputeless banishment,
A fellow of no mark nor likelihood.   45
By being seldom seen, I could not stir
But, like a comet, I was wond'red at;
That men would tell their children, "This is he!"

24, 25. **Which…newsmongers:** which great persons must of necessity often hear by the report of smiling parasites and base talebearers.—**pickthanks.** To *pick a thank* is an idiom for to "speak or act merely for the sake of winning one's favor." The noun is common in the sense of "flatterer" or "parasite," especially one who pretends to give secret information. Holinshed tells us that the Prince "got knowledge that certeine of his fathers seruants were busie to giue informations against him…: they put into the kings head, not onlie what euill rule [i.e., conduct] (according to the course of youth) the prince kept…, but also what great resort of people came to his house.…These tales brought no small suspicion into the kings head, least his sonne would presume to vsurpe the crowne." Holinshed styles these informers "pickthanks." 28. **on my true submission:** when I submit myself in all sincerity to your judgment. 29. **God pardon thee!** I pardon thee, and I pray that God will pardon thee also. 30, 31. **affections:** inclinations.—**hold a wing.** A figure from falconry.—**from.** The emphatic *from:* "away from," "contrary to." 32. **rudely lost:** lost by thy rude conduct. According to Holinshed the Prince "had with his fist striken the cheefe justice for sending one of his minions…to prison." "The king after expelled him out of his priuie councell, banisht him the court, and made the duke of Clarence (his yoonger brother) president of councell in his steed." 36. **time:** thy time of life; thy youth. 38. **do.** The form of the verb is determined by the general sense of plurality in the preceding phrase. 40. **So common-hackney'd…men:** made such an ordinary sight for everybody's eyes. A *hackney* is a horse kept for hire. 42, 43. **Opinion:** public opinion.—**Had:** would have.—**possession:** the possessor—King Richard. Abstract nouns are often used to designate persons. 45. **likelihood:** promise. 46 ff. King Henry is so earnest in his desire for his son's reformation that he exposes his own politic course of action in bringing about the deposition of Richard II.

Others would say, 'Where? Which is Bolingbroke?'
And then I stole all courtesy from heaven,   50
And dress'd myself in such humility
That I did pluck allegiance from men's hearts,
Loud shouts and salutations from their mouths
Even in the presence of the crowned King.
Thus did I keep my person fresh and new,   55
My presence, like a robe pontifical,
Ne'er seen but wond'red at; and so my state,
Seldom but sumptuous, show'd like a feast
And won by rareness such solemnity.
The skipping King, he ambled up and down   60
With shallow jesters and rash bavin wits,
Soon kindled and soon burnt; carded his state;
Mingled his royalty with cap'ring fools;
Had his great name profaned with their scorns
And gave his countenance, against his name,   65
To laugh at gibing boys and stand the push
Of every beardless vain comparative;
Grew a companion to the common streets,
Enfeoff'd himself to popularity;
That, being daily swallowed by men's eyes,   70
They surfeited with honey and began
To loathe the taste of sweetness, whereof a little
More than a little is by much too much.
So, when he had occasion to be seen,
He was but as the cuckoo is in June,   75
Heard, not regarded—seen, but with such eyes
As, sick and blunted with community,
Afford no extraordinary gaze,

---

50. **I stole all courtesy from heaven:** I assumed in my bearing a courtesy like that of heaven. The King is thinking of the doctrine that all men are of equal rank in God's sight—that "God is no respecter of persons" (*Acts*, x, 34). *Stole* expresses the hypocrisy of his conduct. 51. **dress'd myself.** Figures from clothing abound in Shakespeare. 56. **pontifical:** such as is worn on solemn occasions by the Pope or an archbishop. 57–59. **my state:** the splendor that marked the occasions when I appeared in state.— **show'd like a feast:** resembled a great feast day—a solemn festival.—**such solemnity:** i.e., such as attends a festival. *Such* is emphatic. 60, 61. **up and down:** everywhere; hither and yon—always in public sight.—**rash bavin wits:** flashy. Explained by what follows: "soon kindled and soon burnt." *Rash* means "quick." A *bavin* is a fagot of brushwood used for kindling. 62. **carded his state:** debased his royal dignity by associating with such fellows. To *card* is to "adulterate." The figure seems to come from mixing coarse wool with fine in the process of carding (combing out with the instrument called a "card"). 64. **with their scorns:** by their scoffs and taunts. 65. **countenance:** authority. —**name:** reputation. 66, 67. **gibing:** making satirical jests.—**stand the push...comparative:** meet, on equal terms, the onset of every empty-headed youngster who displays his wit in making satirical comparisons. 69. **Enfeoff'd himself to popularity:** gave himself to the common people as their absolute possession. 70. **That:** so that. 75. **in June:** when cuckoos abound. 77. **with community:** by the commonness of the sight.

Such as is bent on sunlike majesty
When it shines seldom in admiring eyes;   80
But rather drows'd and hung their eyelids down,
Slept in his face, and rend'red such aspect
As cloudy men use to their adversaries,
Being with his presence glutted, gorg'd, and full.
And in that very line, Harry, standest thou;   85
For thou hast lost thy princely privilege
With vile participation. Not an eye
But is aweary of thy common sight,
Save mine, which hath desir'd to see thee more;
Which now doth that I would not have it do—   90
Make blind itself with foolish tenderness.

PRINCE.   I shall hereafter, my thrice-gracious lord,
Be more myself.

KING.   For all the world,
As thou art to this hour, was Richard then
When I from France set foot at Ravenspurgh;   95
And even as I was then is Percy now.
Now, by my sceptre, and my soul to boot,
He hath more worthy interest to the state
Than thou, the shadow of succession;
For of no right, nor color like to right,   100
He doth fill fields with harness in the realm,
Turns head against the lion's armed jaws,
And, being no more in debt to years than thou,
Leads ancient lords and reverend bishops on
To bloody battles and to bruising arms.   105
What never-dying honor hath he got
Against renowmed Douglas! whose high deeds,
Whose hot incursions and great name in arms
Holds from all soldiers chief majority
And military title capital   110
Through all the kingdoms that acknowledge Christ.

---

82. **such aspéct:** such a look. 83. **cloudy:** sullen, frowning. 87. **With vile participation:** by associating (prince though thou art) with worthless companions. 93. **For all the world:** in every respect. 98. **more worthy interest to the state:** a more valid claim to the kingdom. 99. **thou...succession:** *thou,* who art but the shadow of my successor—for thy claim has no substantial background of merit. 100–102. **color:** pretext.—**harness:** men in armor.—**Turns head:** marches with an armed troop.—**the lion's armed jaws:** the King's army. 103. **no more.** Shakespeare takes felicitous liberty with dates. Percy was, in fact, of about the same age as King Henry. 107. **renowmed:** renowned. 109, 110. **majority:** preëminence.—**capital:** of highest rank.

Henry IV (John Gielgud) chastising his son Hal (Keith Baxter). (Welles's *Chimes at Midnight*)

Thrice hath this Hotspur, Mars in swathling clothes,
This infant warrior, in his enterprises
Discomfited great Douglas; ta'en him once,
Enlarged him, and made a friend of him,   115
To fill the mouth of deep defiance up
And shake the peace and safety of our throne.
And what say you to this? Percy, Northumberland,
The Archbishop's Grace of York, Douglas, Mortimer
Capitulate against us and are up.   120
But wherefore do I tell these news to thee?
Why, Harry, do I tell thee of my foes,
Which art my nearest and dearest enemy?
Thou that art like enough, through vassal fear,
Base inclination, and the start of spleen,   125
To fight against me under Percy's pay,
To dog his heels and curtsy at his frowns,
To show how much thou art degenerate.

---

112. **swathling:** swaddling. 115. **Enlarged:** released, freed. 116. **To fill...up:** in order to make his own power to defy us complete. 119. 120. **Capitulate:** have come to an agreement.—**up:** in arms. 121. **these news.** *News* is often plural (*res novae,* "new things"). 123. **dearest.** In a double sense—"best beloved" and "bitterest." *Dear* is often used to emphasize the meaning of the noun that it limits. 124, 125. **like:** likely.—**vassal:** befitting one of low rank. —**Base inclination:** an inclination for baseness—for all that is contemptible.—**the start of spleen:** mere unreasoning impulse; mere caprice.

Henry IV (Michael Cronin) and Hal (Michael Pennington) in an awkward reconciliation. (ESC-TV)

PRINCE.   Do not think so. You shall not find it so.[†]
And God forgive them that so much have sway'd   130
Your Majesty's good thoughts away from me!
I will redeem all this on Percy's head
And, in the closing of some glorious day,
Be bold to tell you that I am your son,
When I will wear a garment all of blood,   135
And stain my favors in a bloody mask,
Which, wash'd away, shall scour my shame with it.
And that shall be the day, whene'er it lights,
That this same child of honor and renown,
This gallant Hotspur, this all-praised knight,   140
And your unthought-of Harry chance to meet.
For every honor sitting on his helm,
Would they were multitudes, and on my head
My shames redoubled! For the time will come

prove himself to his father — when he defeats Hotspur his good
deeds
will
transfer
to him

132. **redeem…head:** make Percy pay for all my faults, with an echo of Hal's pledge to "redeem time" at the end of 1.2. [s.c.] 136. **favours:** features. 137. **my shame:** my disgrace.

† How confident is the actor playing Hal in being able to deliver on his promise to his father here? In the ESC production, Hal (Michael Pennington) is emotionally twisted in knots during this exchange with the king (Michael Cronin). When the scene ends and the king exits, he kicks his father's desk in frustration that he has not achieved the reconciliation he has sought. [s.c.]

That I shall make this Northern youth exchange   145
His glorious deeds for my indignities.
Percy is but my factor, good my lord,
To engross up glorious deeds on my behalf;
And I will call him to so strict account
That he shall render every glory up,   150
Yea, even the slightest worship of his time,
Or I will tear the reckoning from his heart.
This in the name of God I promise here;
The which if he be pleas'd I shall perform,
I do beseech your Majesty may salve   155
The long-grown wounds of my intemperance.
If not, the end of life cancels all bands,
And I will die a hundred thousand deaths
Ere break the smallest parcel of this vow.

KING.   A hundred thousand rebels die in this!   160
Thou shalt have charge and sovereign trust herein.

Enter Blunt.

How now, good Blunt? Thy looks are full of speed.

BLUNT.   So hath the business that I come to speak of.
Lord Mortimer of Scotland hath sent word
That Douglas and the English rebels met   165
The eleventh of this month at Shrewsbury.
A mighty and a fearful head they are,
If promises be kept on every hand,
As ever off'red foul play in a state.

KING.   The Earl of Westmoreland set forth today;   170
With him my son, Lord John of Lancaster;
For this advertisement is five days old.
On Wednesday next, Harry, you shall set forward;

---

146. **my indignities:** my unworthy actions; "my shames" (line 144). 147, 148. **factor:** agent.—**engross up:** to buy up *in gross* (i.e., as we say, "wholesale") so as to control ("corner") the market. The mercantile imagery here indicates Hal is prepared to enter his father's business. [s.c.] 150. **render every glory.** The idea is that one who subdues a champion succeeds to all the honors that the champion has won. Percy, at the moment of death, subscribes to this doctrine (5. 4. 77–80). 151. **worship:** honor.—**time:** lifetime. 156. **intemperance:** wild or dissolute behaviour. 157. **cancels all bands:** all bonds. One cannot collect a debt from a dead man: he has "paid the debt of nature." 159. **parcel:** part. 161. **charge:** a charge of soldiers; a commission. 163. **So hath...of:** And, in like manner, the business that I come to report *hath speed*—i.e., requires immediate action. 164. **Lord Mortimer of Scotland:** George Dunbar, the Scottish Earl of March. Shakespeare calls him Mortimer because the Mortimers were Earls of March in England. The *March* was the "Border"—the region immediately north and south of the boundary line between the two kingdoms. 167. **head:** armed force. 169. **foul play.** The opposite of "fair play"—not restricted, as in modern usage, to murder. Here it is used for "rebellion" or "treason." 172. **advértisement:** information, news.

On Thursday we ourselves will march. Our meeting
Is Bridgenorth; and, Harry, you shall march   175
Through Gloucestershire; by which account,
Our business valued, some twelve days hence
Our general forces at Bridgenorth shall meet.
Our hands are full of business. Let's away.
Advantage feeds him fat while men delay.   *Exeunt.*

SCENE III. [*Eastcheap. The Boar's Head Tavern.*]

Enter Falstaff *and* Bardolph.

FAL.   Bardolph, am I not fall'n away vilely since this last action? Do I not
            bate? Do I not dwindle? Why, my skin hangs about me like an old
            lady's loose gown! I am withered like an old apple John. Well, I'll
            repent, and that suddenly, while I am in some liking. I shall be out of
            heart shortly, and then I shall have no strength to repent. An I have not
            forgotten what the inside of a church is made of, I am a peppercorn, a
            brewer's horse. The inside of a church! Company, villanous company,
            hath been the spoil of me.‡

BARD.   Sir John, you are so fretful you cannot live long.   9

FAL.   Why, there is it! Come, sing me a bawdy song; make me merry. I was
            as virtuously given as a gentleman need to be, virtuous enough: swore
            little, dic'd not above seven times a week, went to a bawdy house not
            above once in a quarter—of an hour, paid money that I borrowed—
            three or four times, lived well, and in good compass; and now I live
            out of all order, out of all compass.   15

175. **Bridgenorth:** in Shropshire, on the Severn, not far from Shrewsbury. 176, 177. **by which account:**
by which reckoning—i.e., according to this computation of time.—**Our business valued:** considering
the time that our preparation will require. The absolute construction. 180. **him:** himself.
SCENE III
We are back in the Boar's Head tavern in Eastcheap. 1, 2. **fallen away:** shrunk.—**this last action:** the
robbery at Gad's Hill. Falstaff speaks of it as a military encounter.—**bate:** abate, grow thin. 3–5. **apple
John:** a kind of apple that was not mellow until it had been kept for some time. The skin became loose
and shrivelled in storage. **suddenly:** immediately.—**while...liking:** while I have some flesh. *In good
liking* is an old phrase for "in substantial bodily condition."—**out of heart:** depressed in mind and
body; in a decline. 7. **a brewer...horse.** Brewers' horses were old and worn-out creatures—not fit for
riding. 9. **you are so fretful...long:** you'll fret yourself to death. 10–11. **there is it:** That's just what the
matter is.—**given:** inclined. 14. **in good compass:** within proper limits (of conduct). Bardolph's pun
was inevitable. He applies *compass* in the literal sense of "circumference," "girth."

‡   In the ESC production Falstaff (Barry Stanton) is nursing a mighty hangover as this scene begins.
      When he asks Bardolph to sing him a bawdy song, Bardolph (Colin Farrell) responds by playing a
      loud blast on his trombone. The trombone is repeatedly associated with Falstaff in the production
      as is the flute with Hal reminding us of the potential for the use of music when translating
      Shakespeare from the page to the stage or screen. [s.c.]

BARD.   Why, you are so fat, Sir John, that you must needs be out of all
          compass—out of all reasonable compass, Sir John.

FAL.   Do thou amend thy face, and I'll amend my life. Thou art our admiral,
          thou bearest the lantern in the poop—but 'tis in the nose of thee. Thou
          art the Knight of the Burning Lamp.   20

BARD.   Why, Sir John, my face does you no harm.

FAL.   No, I'll be sworn. I make as good use of it as many a man doth of a
          death's-head or a memento mori. I never see thy face but I think upon
          hellfire and Dives that lived in purple; for there he is in his robes,
          burning, burning. If thou wert any way given to virtue, I would swear
          by thy face; my oath should be "By this fire, that's God's angel." But
          thou art altogether given over, and wert indeed, but for the light in
          thy face, the son of utter darkness. When thou ran'st up Gadshill in
          the night to catch my horse, if I did not think thou hadst been an
          ignis fatuus or a ball of wildfire, there's no purchase in money. O, thou
          art a perpetual triumph, an everlasting bonfire-light! Thou hast saved
          me a thousand marks in links and torches, walking with thee in the
          night betwixt tavern and tavern; but the sack that thou hast drunk me
          would have bought me lights as good cheap at the dearest chandler's in
          Europe. I have maintained that salamander of yours with fire any time
          this two-and-thirty years. God reward me for it!   36

BARD.   'Sblood, I would my face were in your belly!

FAL.   God-a-mercy! so should I be sure to be heart-burn'd.

---

18. **our admiral:** our flagship. The admiral's ship took the lead and therefore had a light in the stern.
20. **the Knight of the Burning Lamp.** A title made up in imitation of the names taken by adventurous
knights in the romances of chivalry. They were regularly derived from the device on the shield: Knight
of the Sun; of the Lion; of the Swan, etc. 22. **as good use of it:** i.e., as a warning of death and the last
judgment. The figure of a skull (or skull and crossbones) served as a *memento mori*, i.e., as a reminder
of the inevitability of death. Such an emblem was often engraved on the seal of a ring. 24. **Dives:** the
"rich man" in *Luke*, xvi, 19 ff. 26–28. **By this fire...angel.** *Psalm* civ, 4: "Who maketh his angels
spirits; his ministers a flaming fire."—**given over:** i.e., to Satan.—**utter darkness:** outer darkness.
Another Biblical allusion. See *Matthew*, xxv, 30: "And cast ye the unprofitable servant into utter
darkness: there shall be weeping and gnashing of teeth." Falstaff often quotes Scripture or uses religious
phraseology. Everybody knew his Bible. Nothing was commoner, for instance, than for a lawyer to
appeal to scriptural authority in an argument in court. 30–35. **ignis fatuus:** fool's fire; will-o'-the-
wisp.—**wildfire:** a kind of firework used in war. The term was also applied to fiery appearances in
the air, which were often thought to be evil spirits.—**there's no purchase in money:** money is not
worth stealing. *Purchase* means "booty."—**triumph:** illumination, as at a public festival.—**marks.** A
mark was two thirds of a pound.—**links:** small torches. There were no street lights. Linkboys were
hired if the night was dark.—**as good cheap:** as cheap—literally, at as favourable a market (*à bon
marché*).—**chandler:** candle-maker.—**salamander:** a fabulous lizard that lived in the element of fire
and made fire its food. 37. **'Sblood.** See 1.2.56, note.—**I would...belly.** A proverbial curse on a bore
or an impertinent talker. "I wish that word (or that subject) had been swallowed by you, so that I need
hear no more of it." There is an implication that the morsel would be indigestible. Compare the phrase
"to eat one's words." 38. **God-a-mercy:** God have mercy.—**heart-burn'd.** *Heartburn* is an old name for
a certain symptom of indigestion. It is caused by acid from the stomach.

Enter Hostess.

How now, Dame Partlet the hen? Have you enquir'd yet who pick'd my
pocket? 40

HOST. Why, Sir John, what do you think, Sir John? Do you think I keep
thieves in my house? I have search'd, I have enquired, so has my
husband, man by man, boy by boy, servant by servant. The tithe of a
hair was never lost in my house before.

FAL. Ye lie, hostess. Bardolph was shav'd and lost many a hair, and I'll be
sworn my pocket was pick'd. Go to, you are a woman, go! 46

HOST. Who, I? No; I defy thee! God's light, I was never call'd so in mine own
house before!

FAL. Go to, I know you well enough.

HOST. No, Sir John; you do not know me, Sir John. I know you, Sir John.
You owe me money, Sir John, and now you pick a quarrel to beguile
me of it. I bought you a dozen of shirts to your back. 52

FAL. Dowlas, filthy dowlas! I have given them away to bakers' wives; they
have made bolters of them.

HOST. Now, as I am a true woman, holland of eight shillings an ell. You owe
money here besides, Sir John, for your diet and by-drinkings, and
money lent you, four-and-twenty pound.

FAL. He had his part of it; let him pay.

HOST. He? Alas, he is poor; he hath nothing. 59

FAL. How? Poor? Look upon his face. What call you rich? Let them coin
his nose, let them coin his cheeks. I'll not pay a denier. What, will you
make a younker of me? Shall I not take mine ease in mine inn but I
shall have my pocket pick'd? I have lost a seal-ring of my grandfather's
worth forty mark. 64

HOST. O Jesu, I have heard the Prince tell him, I know not how oft, that that
ring was copper!

FAL. How? the Prince is a Jack, a sneak-cup. 'Sblood, an he were here, I
would cudgel him like a dog if he would say so.

---

39. **Dame Partlet.** Pertelote is the name of the hen in Chaucer's *Nun's Priest's Tale.* The Hostess's manner
is that of a startled and fluttering fowl. Note her agitated entrance at 2.4.221. 43. **the tithe:** the tenth
part. 46. **Go to:** Away with you! 47. **God's light.** A common oath, often abbreviated to *'Slight.* 53–54.
dowlas: a kind of coarse linen.—**bolters:** cloths for sifting flour. 52–56. **holland:** fine linen.—**an ell:** a
cloth measure of forty-five inches.—**by-drinkings:** drinks between meals. 61. **denier:** the least coin. A
denier (Latin *denarius*) was a French coin of small value. 62. **a younker:** an unsophisticated youngster.
64. **mark.** See line 43. 67. **Jack:** a low fellow; a rascal.—**a sneak-cup:** one who "sneaks drinks"—does
not drink glass for glass with his friends.

Enter the Prince [*and* Poins], *marching; and* Falstaff *meets them, playing upon his truncheon like a fife.*

How now, lad? Is the wind in that door, i' faith? Must we all march?

BARD. Yea, two and two, Newgate fashion. 70

HOST. My lord, I pray you hear me.

PRINCE. What say'st thou, Mistress Quickly?
How doth thy husband? I love him well; he is an honest man.

HOST. Good my lord, hear me.

FAL. Prithee let her alone and list to me. 75

PRINCE. What say'st thou, Jack?

FAL. The other night I fell asleep here behind the arras and had my pocket pick'd. This house is turn'd bawdy house; they pick pockets.

PRINCE. What didst thou lose, Jack? 79

FAL. Wilt thou believe me, Hal? Three or four bonds of forty pound apiece and a seal-ring of my grandfather's.

PRINCE. A trifle, some eightpenny matter.

HOST. So I told him, my lord, and I said I heard your Grace say so; and, my lord, he speaks most vilely of you, like a foul-mouth'd man as he is, and said he would cudgel you. 85

PRINCE. What! he did not?

HOST. There's neither faith, truth, nor womanhood in me else.

FAL. There's no more faith in thee than in a stewed prune, nor no more truth in thee than in a drawn fox; and for womanhood, Maid Marian may be the deputy's wife of the ward to thee. Go, you thing, go! 90

HOST. Say, what thing? what thing?

FAL. What thing? Why, a thing to thank God on.

HOST. I am no thing to thank God on, I would thou shouldst know it! I am an honest man's wife, and, setting thy knighthood aside, thou art a knave to call me so. 95

---

69. **truncheon:** short staff.—**Is...door?** Is that the way the wind blows? 70. **Newgate fashion:** handcuffed or tied together in pairs, like prisoners who are led to Newgate prison or from Newgate to the courtroom. 88. **a stewed prune.** Stewed prunes were a customary dish in houses of ill fame. 89. **a drawn fox:** a fox drawn from his cover, who relies on his cunning to escape the hounds. [S.C.]—**for:** as for. 89–90. **Maid Marian...to thee:** Maid Marian may serve as a pattern of womanly propriety in comparison with you. Maid Marian was a character in May games and morris dances, in which she is sometimes paired with Robin Hood; but she is unknown to the oldest Robin Hood tradition. The girl who played Maid Marian was not likely to be a very decorous person. The *deputy of the ward* was an important local official, and his wife would doubtless be a model of propriety. 92. **on:** for. 94. **setting thy knighthood aside:** if we disregard the fact that you are a knight.

FAL.	Setting thy womanhood aside, thou art a beast to say otherwise.
HOST.	Say, what beast, thou knave, thou?
FAL.	What beast? Why, an otter.
PRINCE.	An otter, Sir John? Why an otter?
FAL.	Why, she's neither fish nor flesh; a man knows not where to have her.
HOST.	Thou art an unjust man in saying so. 101 Thou or any man knows where to have me, thou knave, thou!
PRINCE.	Thou say'st true, hostess, and he slanders thee most grossly.
HOST.	So he doth you, my lord, and said this other day you ought him a thousand pound. 105
PRINCE.	Sirrah, do I owe you a thousand pound?
FAL.	A thousand pound, Hal? A million! Thy love is worth a million; thou owest me thy love.
HOST.	Nay, my lord, he call'd you Jack and said he would cudgel you.
FAL.	Did I, Bardolph? 110
BARD.	Indeed, Sir John, you said so.
FAL.	Yea, if he said my ring was copper.
PRINCE.	I say 'tis copper. Darest thou be as good as thy word now?
FAL.	Why, Hal, thou knowest, as thou art but man, I dare; but as thou art Prince, I fear thee as I fear the roaring of the lion's whelp. 115
PRINCE.	And why not as the lion?
FAL.	The King himself is to be feared as the lion. Dost thou think I'll fear thee as I fear thy father? Nay, an I do, I pray God my girdle break.
PRINCE.	O, if it should, how would thy guts fall about thy knees! But, sirrah, there's no room for faith, truth, nor honesty in this bosom of thine. It is all fill'd up with guts and midriff. Charge an honest woman with picking thy pocket? Why, thou whoreson, impudent, emboss'd rascal, if there were anything in thy pocket but tavern reckonings, memorandums of bawdy houses, and one poor pennyworth of sugar candy to make thee long-winded—if thy pocket were enrich'd with any

---

100. **neither fish nor flesh:** neither one thing nor another. Falstaff refers to Dame Quickly's mental unsteadiness—her inability to stick to the point.—**where to have her:** how to understand her; how to keep track of her talk, with a sexual innuendo. [s.c.] 104. **you.** Emphatic. This is an excellent instance of the Hostess's jumping from one subject to another.—**ought:** owed. 114. **as...man:** insofar as you are merely *man.* 118. **I pray...break.** Often used in asseverations. The misfortune invoked as a penalty for falsehood is obvious enough. There is no mysterious meaning involved. 121. **midriff:** diaphragm. 122. **emboss'd:** swollen.

other injuries but these, I am a villain. And yet you will stand to it; you will not pocket up wrong. Art thou not ashamed?   127

FAL.   Dost thou hear, Hal? Thou knowest in the state of innocency Adam fell; and what should poor Jack Falstaff do in the days of villany? Thou seest I have more flesh than another man, and therefore more frailty. You confess then, you pick'd my pocket?   131

PRINCE. It appears so by the story.

FAL.   Hostess, I forgive thee. Go make ready breakfast. Love thy husband, look to thy servants, cherish thy guests. Thou shalt find me tractable to any honest reason. Thou seest I am pacified.—Still?—Nay, prithee be gone. (*Exit Hostess.*) Now, Hal, to the news at court. For the robbery, lad—how is that answered?

PRINCE. O my sweet beef, I must still be good angel to thee. The money is paid back again.

FAL.   O, I do not like that paying back! 'Tis a double labor.   140

PRINCE. I am good friends with my father, and may do anything.

FAL.   Rob me the exchequer the first thing thou doest, and do it with unwash'd hands too.

BARD.   Do, my lord.

PRINCE. I have procured thee, Jack, a charge of foot.   145

FAL.   I would it had been of horse. Where shall I find one that can steal well? O for a fine thief of the age of two-and-twenty or thereabouts! I am heinously unprovided. Well, God be thanked for these rebels. They offend none but the virtuous. I laud them, I praise them.

PRINCE. Bardolph!   150

BARD.   My lord?

PRINCE. Go bear this letter to Lord John of Lancaster,
         To my brother John; this to my Lord of Westmoreland.[*Exit Bardolph.*]
         Go, Poins, to horse, to horse; for thou and I
         Have thirty miles to ride yet ere dinner time.   [*Exit Poins.*]
         Jack, meet me tomorrow in the Temple Hall   156

126–127. **injuries:** things the loss of which would be an injury to thee. The Prince uses the word in this unusual sense for the sake of a pun on *wrong.*—**pocket.** To *pocket up wrong* is to "accept insults or injuries without protest or resentment," as if they were one's due. 129–130. **in the days of villany:** in the wicked times in which we live.—**more frailty.** Falstaff applies a well-worn proverb that seems to be of Biblical origin (see *Psalms,* xxxix, 4; *Matthew,* xxvi, 41). 135–137. **Still?** Not yet gone? Still in a temper? The Hostess would like to "have the last word," but she is dumbfounded by Falstaff's "I forgive thee," which turns the tables completely.—**For:** as for.—**answered:** settled. 143. **with unwash'd hands:** without stopping to wash your hands. A cant phrase for "without a moment's delay." 145. **a charge of foot.** See 2.4.434. 148. **unprovided:** i.e., with what I need for the campaign.

At two o'clock in the afternoon.
There shalt thou know thy charge, and there receive
Money and order for their furniture.
The land is burning; Percy stands on high;   160
And either they or we must lower lie.   [*Exit.*]

FAL.   Rare words! brave world! Hostess, my breakfast, come.
O, I could wish this tavern were my drum!   *Exit.*

ACT IV

SCENE I. [*The rebel camp near Shrewsbury.*]

Enter Harry Hotspur, Worcester, *and* Douglas.

HOT.   Well said, my noble Scot. If speaking truth
In this fine age were not thought flattery,
Such attribution should the Douglas have
As not a soldier of this season's stamp
Should go so general current through the world.   5
By God, I cannot flatter, I defy
The tongues of soothers! but a braver place
In my heart's love hath no man than yourself.
Nay, task me to my word; approve me, lord.

DOUG.   Thou art the king of honor   10
No man so potent breathes upon the ground
But I will beard him.

Enter one with letters.

HOT.   Do so, and 'tis well.—
What letters hast thou there?—I can but thank you.

---

159. **furniture:** furnishings, equipment. 160. **burning:** on fire with war. 162. **brave:** glorious. 163. **I could wish...my drum:** I could wish this tavern were the only drum that I must follow—that I could come to this tavern instead of following the drum to the field of battle.
ACT IV. SCENE I.
The rebel camp near Shrewsbury. 1. **Well said.** The scene opens near the end of a conversation. 3–5. **attribution:** tribute of praise.—**As:** that.—**stamp:** coinage.—**go so general current:** pass current so universally; be accepted as the supreme soldier. 6, 7. **defy...of soothers:** solemnly renounce such language as flatterers use.—**braver:** finer, more distinguished. 9. **task me to:** call upon me to verify.—**approve me:** put me to the test. 12. **But:** but that.—**beard him:** meet him face to face in combat. 13. **What letters,** etc. Hotspur interrupts himself and then finishes what he had to say to Douglas. Cf. 2.3.56–64.

MESS.   These letters come from your father.

HOT.   Letters from him? Why comes he not himself?   15

MESS.   He cannot come, my lord; he is grievous sick.

HOT.   Zounds! how has he the leisure to be sick
          In such a justling time? Who leads his power?
          Under whose government come they along?

MESS.   His letters bears his mind, not I, my lord.   20

WOR.   I prithee tell me, doth he keep his bed?

MESS.   He did, my lord, four days ere I set forth,
          And at the time of my departure thence
          He was much fear'd by his physicians.

WOR.   I would the state of time had first been whole   25
          Ere he by sickness had been visited.
          His health was never better worth than now.

HOT.   Sick now? droop now? This sickness doth infect
          The very lifeblood of our enterprise.
          'Tis catching hither, even to our camp.   30
          He writes me here that inward sickness—
          And that his friends by deputation could not
          So soon be drawn; nor did he think it meet
          To lay so dangerous and dear a trust
          On any soul remov'd but on his own.   35
          Yet doth he give us bold advertisement,
          That with our small conjunction we should on,
          To see how fortune is dispos'd to us;
          For, as he writes, there is no quailing now,
          Because the King is certainly possess'd   40
          Of all our purposes. What say you to it?

WOR.   Your father's sickness is a maim to us.

HOT.   A perilous gash, a very limb lopp'd off.
          And yet, in faith, it is not! His present want

---

14. **These letters:** this letter. 18. **justling:** turbulent.—**his power:** his troops, his army. 24. **fear'd.** To *fear* means to "fear for," to "worry or be anxious about." 25–27. **time:** the times.—**whole:** sound; in health.—**better worth:** more valuable; of greater consequence. 30. **'Tis catching hither:** its contagion reaches here. 31. **inward sickness—**. Hotspur breaks off the sentence to consult the letter, of which he gives the substance in what follows. 32–35. **by deputation…drawn:** could not be mustered by means of any persons serving as his deputies.—**think…his own:** nor did he think it fitting to entrust a business so dangerous and so important to any other person than himself. *Remov'd* means merely "outside (of one's self)." 36. **bold advertisement:** advice to take the risk. 37. **our small conjunction:** the small army that we have already mustered.—**should on:** should go on; should proceed. 38. **fortune.** Fortune is conceived as a person who may be well or ill disposed toward them. 40. **possess'd:** informed. 44–45. **His present want Seems more:** Our lack of his help seems greater now.

Seems more than we shall find it. Were it good   45
To set the exact wealth of all our states
All at one cast? to set so rich a main
On the nice hazard of one doubtful hour?
It were not good; for therein should we read
The very bottom and the soul of hope,   50
The very list, the very utmost bound
Of all our fortunes.

DOUG.   Faith, and so we should;
Where now remains a sweet reversion.
We may boldly spend upon the hope of what
Is to come in.   55
A comfort of retirement lives in this.

HOT.   A rendezvous, a home to fly unto,
If that the devil and mischance look big
Upon the maidenhead of our affairs.

WOR.   But yet I would your father had been here.   60
The quality and hair of our attempt
Brooks no division. It will be thought
By some that know not why he is away,
That wisdom, loyalty, and mere dislike
Of our proceedings kept the Earl from hence.   65
And think how such an apprehension
May turn the tide of fearful faction
And breed a kind of question in our cause.
For well you know we of the off'ring side
Must keep aloof from strict arbitrement,   70
And stop all sight-holes, every loop from whence
The eye of reason may pry in upon us.
This absence of your father's draws a curtain

46–48. **To set...cast?** To stake (risk) the full amount of the possessions of all of us on one cast of the dice.—**main:** stake.—**nice:** precarious, delicate. 49–51. **for therein...fortunes:** for in so doing—in running such a risk—we should perceive and fully understand that we were exhausting our store of hope—that we had nothing more to hope for—since we were staking to the limit the resources of us all.—**the very soul of hope:** all that keeps hope alive.—**list:** limit. Synonymous with *bound*. 53. **Where:** whereas.—**a sweet reversion:** a comforting expectation—literally, a contingent interest in property that is to revert to one in the future. 56. **A comfort of retirement:** a sustaining reliance on a place of refuge. 58–59. **big:** threatening; with a menacing air.—**maidenhead:** maidhood; untried youth; outset. 61–62. **The quality:** the nature.—**hair:** synonymous with *quality*. The figure comes from the texture and color of fur. —**Brooks:** permits, allows of. 64. **apprehension:** idea.—**fearful:** full of fear; timorous.—**breed...cause:** make the cause for which we fight seem somewhat questionable. 69–70. **we of the off'ring side...arbitrement:** we who are taking the offensive (against established authority) must not allow our actions to be strictly judged. 71. **loop:** loophole. 71–72. **from whence...upon us:** by means of which our cause can be scrutinized and laid open to discussion. 73. **draws:** draws aside.

That shows the ignorant a kind of fear
Before not dreamt of.

HOT.   You strain too far.   75
I rather of his absence make this use:
It lends a lustre and more great opinion,
A larger dare to our great enterprise,
Than if the Earl were here; for men must think,
If we, without his help, can make a head   80
To push against a kingdom, with his help
We shall o'erturn it topsy-turvy down.
Yet all goes well; yet all our joints are whole.

DOUG.   As heart can think. There is not such a word
Spoke of in Scotland as this term of fear.   85

Enter Sir Richard Vernon.

HOT.   My cousin Vernon! welcome, by my soul.

VER.   Pray God my news be worth a welcome, lord.
The Earl of Westmoreland, seven thousand strong,
Is marching hitherwards; with him Prince John.

HOT.   No harm. What more?

VER.   And further, I have learn'd   90
The King himself in person is set forth,
Or hitherwards intended speedily,
With strong and mighty preparation.

HOT.   He shall be welcome too. Where is his son,
The nimble-footed madcap Prince of Wales,   95
And his comrades, that daff'd the world aside
And bid it pass?

VER.   All furnish'd, all in arms;
All plum'd like estridges that with the wind
Bated like eagles having lately bath'd;

74–75. **shows...dreamt of:** makes those who do not know the real cause of his absence interpret it as due to some feeling of fear—and that is a weakness that they have never dreamt of ascribing to any of our party.—**strain too far:** exaggerate the danger. 76. **this use:** this application; this interpretation. 77. **opinion:** repute; estimation (on the part of the people). 80. **make a head:** raise an army. 92. **intended:** on the point of setting out. 93. **preparation:** an army ready for the field. 95–96. **nimble-footed.** swift.— **madcap.** Here used as an adjective.—**daff'd...aside:** put away from them; carelessly disregarded. *Daff* (i.e., *doff*) is from *do off,* "put off." 97. **And bid it pass.** "Let the world pass" was a common exclamation of careless revellers: "Don't worry about anything. Enjoy the present moment and let the serious affairs of life take care of themselves." 98–99. **estridges:** ostriches.—**that.** The antecedents are *Prince* and *comrades* (lines 95, 96), not *estridges.*—**Bated:** were flapping their wings, i.e., were displaying their fine array. *Bate* (French *battre*) was a falconer's term.

Glittering in golden coats like images;   *pastoral myth language*   100
As full of spirit as the month of May
And gorgeous as the sun at midsummer;
Wanton as youthful goats, wild as young bulls.
I saw young Harry with his beaver on,
His cushes on his thighs, gallantly arm'd,   105
Rise from the ground like feathered Mercury,   *reborn*
And vaulted with such ease into his seat
As if an angel dropp'd down from the clouds
To turn and wind a fiery Pegasus
And witch the world with noble horsemanship.   110

HOT. *like Richard*   No more, no more! Worse than the sun in March,
This praise doth nourish agues. Let them come.
They come like sacrifices in their trim,
And to the fire-ey'd maid of smoky war   *love to wife -> battlefield*
All hot and bleeding will we offer them.   115
The mailed Mars shall on his altar sit
Up to the ears in blood. I am on fire
To hear this rich reprisal is so nigh,
And yet not ours. Come, let me taste my horse,   *erotically violent*
Who is to bear me like a thunderbolt   *language*   120
Against the bosom of the Prince of Wales.   *(similar to kate 36)*
Harry to Harry shall, hot horse to horse,
Meet, and ne'er part till one drop down a corse.
O that Glendower were come!   *desire for crown -> desire for erotic violence*

VER.   There is more in us
I learn'd in Worcester, as I rode along,   *to the person*   125
He cannot draw his power this fourteen days.

DOUG.   That's the worst tidings that I hear of yet.

WOR.   Ay, by my faith, that bears a frosty sound.

HOT.   What may the King's whole battle reach unto?

VER.   To thirty thousand.

---

100. **images:** images of the saints on holy days. 103. **Wanton:** sportive. 104–105. **beaver:** helmet.—
cushes: cuisses—armor for the thighs. 106. **feathered:** wing-footed. 107. **vaulted:** he vaulted. 109,
110. **wind.** Synonymous with *turn.*—**Pegasus:** the winged horse of ancient myth.—**witch:** bewitch,
charm. 112. **agues.** Malarial fever (fever and ague) was prevalent in Shakespeare's time on account of
the undrained marshes. It was thought to be caused by vapours drawn up from marshland by the sun,
especially in early spring. 113. **in their trim:** in their fine array. 114. **the fire-ey'd maid:** Bellona, the
goddess of war. 118–120. **reprisal:** prize, booty.—**taste:** try.—**a thunderbolt:** a fiery bolt, or stone
missile, supposed to be discharged from the clouds by the thunder and to destroy whatever it strikes.
126. **draw his power:** muster his troops. 129. **battle:** army.

HOT.   Forty let it be.   130
        My father and Glendower being both away,
        The powers of us may serve so great a day.
        Come, let us take a muster speedily.
        Doomsday is near. Die all, die merrily.— is this a moment of clarity?

DOUG.   Talk not of dying. I am out of fear   135
        Of death or death's hand for this one half-year.   *Exeunt.*

SCENE II. [*A public road near Coventry.*]

Enter Falstaff *and* Bardolph.

FAL.   Bardolph, get thee before to Coventry; fill me a bottle of sack. Our
        soldiers shall march through. We'll to Sutton Co'fil' tonight.

BARD.   Will you give me money, Captain?

FAL.   Lay out, lay out.

BARD.   This bottle makes an angel.   5

FAL.   An if it do, take it for thy labor; an if it make twenty, take them all; I'll
        answer the coinage. Bid my lieutenant Peto meet me at town's end.

BARD.   I will, Captain. Farewell.   *Exit.*

FAL.   If I be not ashamed of my soldiers, I am a sous'd gurnet. I have misused
        the King's press damnably. I have got, in exchange of a hundred and
        fifty soldiers, three hundred and odd pounds. I press me none but good
        householders, yeomen's sons; inquire me out contracted bachelors,
        such as had been ask'd twice on the banes—such a commodity of warm
        slaves as had as lieve hear the devil as a drum; such as fear the report
        of a caliver worse than a struck fowl or a hurt wild duck. I press'd me
        none but such toasts-and-butter, with hearts in their bellies no bigger
        than pins' heads, and they have bought out their services; and now my

---

132. **serve:** suffice for.—**so great:** even so great. 134. **Die all...merrily:** If we must all die, let us die
cheerfully.
SCENE II
This scene takes place on the road to Shrewsbury. 2. **Sutton Co'fil':** Sutton Coldfield in Warwickshire,
near Birmingham. 4. **Lay out:** Pay out of your own pocket. 5. **makes an angel:** makes ten shillings that
you owe me. 7. **I'll answer the coinage:** I'll be responsible for any coinage that the bottle does. 9–15.
sous'd gurnet: a small pickled fish and a delicacy. [s.c.]—**press:** conscription, forced enlistment.—
contracted: engaged to be married.—**the banes:** the banns—the announcement of intended marriage,
made in church by the parson, who called upon any who knew of an impediment to the marriage to
speak out. The banns were thus proclaimed on three successive Sundays. After the third proclamation
the marriage could take place.—**commodity:** lot.—**warm slaves:** well-to-do and comfort-loving
fellows.—**lieve:** lief.—**caliver:** a kind of light musket.—**press'd:** impressed, conscripted. 16. **toasts-
and-butter:** delicate feeders, quite unused to soldiers' rough-and-ready fare. 17. **bought out their
services:** paid me money to be released from service. Then Falstaff had proceeded to enlist poverty-
stricken recruits in their place.

whole charge consists of ancients, corporals, lieutenants, gentlemen of
companies—slaves as ragged as Lazarus in the painted cloth, where the
glutton's dogs licked his sores; and such as indeed were never soldiers,
but discarded unjust servingmen, younger sons to younger brothers,
revolted tapsters, and ostlers trade-fall'n; the cankers of a calm world
and a long peace; ten times more dishonorable ragged than an old fac'd
ancient; and such have I to fill up the rooms of them that have bought
out their services that you would think that I had a hundred and
fifty tattered Prodigals lately come from swine-keeping, from eating
draff and husks. A mad fellow met me on the way, and told me I had
unloaded all the gibbets and press'd the dead bodies. No eye hath seen
such scarecrows. I'll not march through Coventry with them, that's
flat. Nay, and the villains march wide betwixt the legs, as if they had
gyves on; for indeed I had the most of them out of prison. There's but
a shirt and a half in all my company; and the half-shirt is two napkins
tack'd together and thrown over the shoulders like a herald's coat
without sleeves; and the shirt, to say the truth, stol'n from my host at
Saint Alban's, or the red-nose innkeeper of Daventry. But that's all one;
they'll find linen enough on every hedge.†   36

Enter the Prince *and the* Lord of Westmoreland.

PRINCE.   How now, blown Jack? How now, quilt?

18–22. **charge:** company.—**of ancients:** of ensigns literally, standard-bearers. Discharged soldiers
had a hard lot in old times. They often took to begging or robbery for a livelihood. —**gentlemen of
companies.** An old technical term for a soldier (apparently a volunteer) who was superior to an ordinary
private and yet not definitely an officer. His precise rank, indeed, was always a matter of dispute.
Lazarus. The beggar in the Dives parable. See *Luke*, xvi, 19 ff.—**painted cloth.** A cheap substitute for
tapestry hangings.—**and such as:** and, besides, of others who, etc.—**discarded:** discharged.—**unjust:**
dishonest.—**revolted tapsters:** runaway wine-waiters.—**trade-fall'n:** fallen away from their trade; out of
business.—**cankers:** canker-worms; creatures that are bred in time of peace and prey upon the public.
23–24. **more dishonourable ragged than an old fac'd ancient:** more ragged than an old patched
flag—and dishonourable in their raggedness. *Dishonourable* does not apply to the flag but only to these
vagabonds. *Ancient* in this sense is merely a mispronounced form of *ensign*. 27. **draff:** garbage. The prodigal
son, in *Luke*, xv, 11 ff., was so hungry that he longed for draff. [s.c.] 30–36. **villains:** a general term of
contempt.—**gyves:** fetters.—**out of prison.** It was common to release convicts on condition of their
enlisting.—**a herald's coat without sleeves:** a so-called *tabard*—a loose sleeveless coat, the uniform of a
herald.—**that's all one:** that makes no difference; that's no matter.—**on every hedge:** where it was spread
to dry or bleach. 37. **blown:** puffed up, swollen. —**quilt:** padded fellow,—literally, a padded coverlet.

---

†   Anthony Quayle's Falstaff in the BBC version is not dressed in military uniform but wears a comic
metal helmet with the ear flaps turned up. He delivers his description of his troops in close-up
directly to the camera becoming the audience's confidante. In contrast, Barry Stanton, in the
ESC version, is dressed in full military regalia (looking like one of the Buckingham Palace horse
guards) and sits on his tavern chair now mounted on a cart being pulled by Bardolph. Quayle's
Falstaff as something of a choric commentator providing the perspective of the common man;
Stanton's Falstaff is a slightly seedy aristocrat looking to make the most out of the turmoil of
military confrontation. [s.c.]

FAL.   What, Hal? How now, mad wag? What a devil dost thou in
Warwickshire? My good Lord of Westmoreland, I cry you mercy. I
thought your honor had already been at Shrewsbury.   40

WEST.   Faith, Sir John, 'tis more than time that I were there, and you too; but
my powers are there already. The King, I can tell you, looks for us all.
We must away all, tonight.

FAL.   Tut, never fear me. I am as vigilant as a cat to steal cream.

PRINCE.   I think, to steal cream indeed, for thy theft hath already made thee
butter. But tell me, Jack, whose fellows are these that come after?   46

FAL.   Mine, Hal, mine.

PRINCE.   I did never see such pitiful rascals.

FAL.   Tut, tut! good enough to toss; food for powder, food for powder.
They'll fill a pit as well as better. Tush, man, mortal men, mortal men.

WEST.   Ay, but, Sir John, methinks they are exceeding poor and bare—too
beggarly.   52

FAL.   Faith, for their poverty, I know not where they had that; and for their
bareness, I am sure they never learn'd that of me.

PRINCE.   No, I'll be sworn, unless you call three fingers on the ribs bare. But,
sirrah, make haste. Percy is already in the field.   [*Exit.*]   56

FAL.   What, is the King encamp'd?

WEST.   He is, Sir John. I fear we shall stay too long.   [*Exit.*]

FAL.   Well, to the latter end of a fray and the beginning of a feast
Fits a dull fighter and a keen guest.   *Exit.*   60

SCENE III. [*The rebel camp near Shrewsbury.*]

Enter Hotspur, Worcester, Douglas, Vernon.

HOT.   We'll fight with him tonight.

WOR.   It may not be.

DOUG.   You give him then advantage.

VER.   Not a whit.

38–39. **mad wag:** wild fellow.—**I cry you mercy:** I beg your pardon (for seeming to overlook you). 42.
powers: troops. 44. **never fear me:** don't be worried about me. 49. **to toss:** for tossing on a pike. 53. **for:**
as for. 59–60. Falstaff adapts an old proverb, "It is better coming to the beginning of a feast than the end
of a fray" to remind us that his appetite is for pleasure while Westmoreland's is for war. [S.C.]
SCENE III
The rebel camp near Shrewsbury.

HOT.	Why say you so? Looks he not for supply?
VER.	So do we.
HOT.	His is certain, ours is doubtful.
WOR.	Good cousin, be advis'd; stir not tonight.

5

VER.	Do not, my lord.
DOUG.	You do not counsel well.
	You speak it out of fear and cold heart.

VER.   Do me no slander, Douglas. By my life—
And I dare well maintain it with my life—
If well-respected honor bid me on,   10
I hold as little counsel with weak fear
As you, my lord, or any Scot that this day lives.
Let it be seen tomorrow in the battle
Which of us fears.

DOUG.	Yea, or tonight.
VER.	Content.
HOT.	Tonight, say I.

15

VER.   Come, come, it may not be. I wonder much,
Being men of such great leading as you are,
That you foresee not what impediments
Drag back our expedition. Certain horse
Of my cousin Vernon's are not yet come up.   20
Your uncle Worcester's horse came but today,
And now their pride and mettle is asleep,
Their courage with hard labor tame and dull,
That not a horse is half the half of himself.

HOT.   So are the horses of the enemy,   25
In general journey-bated and brought low.
The better part of ours are full of rest.

WOR.   The number of the King exceedeth ours.
For God's sake, cousin, stay till all come in.

The trumpet sounds a parley. Enter Sir Walter Blunt.

BLUNT.   I come with gracious offers from the King,   30

---

3. **supply:** reinforcements. 5. **be advis'd:** take our advice; listen to reason. 10. **well-respected:** well-considered, i.e., based upon sound principles of conduct. Vernon makes a distinction between honor as thus determined and the fantastic code of foolhardy valor.—**bid me on:** call upon me to go forward. 17. **leading:** experience in leadership in war. 19. **horse:** cavalry. 22. **pride:** spirit. Synonymous with *mettle.* 24. **That:** so that. 26. **journey-bated:** worn out by travel. To *bate* is to "abate."

If you vouchsafe me hearing and respect.

HOT. Welcome, Sir Walter Blunt, and would to God
You were of our determination!
Some of us love you well; and even those some
Envy your great deservings and good name,   35
Because you are not of our quality,
But stand against us like an enemy.

BLUNT. And God defend but still I should stand so,
So long as out of limit and true rule
You stand against anointed majesty!   40
But to my charge. The King hath sent to know
The nature of your griefs; and whereupon
You conjure from the breast of civil peace
Such bold hostility, teaching his duteous land
Audacious cruelty. If that the King   45
Have any way your good deserts forgot,
Which he confesseth to be manifold,
He bids you name your griefs, and with all speed
You shall have your desires with interest,
And pardon absolute for yourself and these   50
Herein misled by your suggestion.

HOT. The King is kind; and well we know the King
Knows at what time to promise, when to pay.
My father and my uncle and myself
Did give him that same royalty he wears;   55
And when he was not six-and-twenty strong,
Sick in the world's regard, wretched and low,
A poor unminded outlaw sneaking home,
My father gave him welcome to the shore;
And when he heard him swear and vow to God   60
He came but to be Duke of Lancaster,
To sue his livery and beg his peace,
With tears of innocency and terms of zeal,

---

31. **respect:** attention. 33. **of our determination:** of our party; on our side. 36. **quality:** party. 38–39.
defend: forbid.—**still:** ever, always.—**limit:** bounds.—**true rule:** right conduct. 41. **my charge:** my
errand; the message entrusted to me. 42–43. **griefs:** grievances.—**whereupon:** for what reason. *On* or
upon was common in a causal sense. This use survives in *on compulsion, on purpose.*—**conjure:** call up,
as it were by magic spells (such as were used to raise devils).—**civil:** well-behaved, orderly. 45. **If that:**
if. 51. **suggestion:** evil suggestion—almost equivalent to "temptation." 56. **not six-and-twenty strong.**
Cf. Holinshed: "and with him not past threescore persons, as some write." 62. **To sue his livery:** to
prove his title and procure the delivery into his own possession of his lands, which were then held by
King Richard. Bolingbroke's father, the Duke of Lancaster, held his lands as tenant of the crown, and
on his death they were (according to law) taken by the King. The heir was obliged to make suit in the
Court of Wards in order to inherit them. 63. **terms of zeal:** protestations of devoted loyalty.

My father, in kind heart and pity mov'd,
Swore him assistance, and perform'd it too.   65
Now when the lords and barons of the realm
Perceiv'd Northumberland did lean to him,
The more and less came in with cap and knee;
Met him in boroughs, cities, villages,
Attended him on bridges, stood in lanes,   70
Laid gifts before him, proffer'd him their oaths,
Gave him their heirs as pages, followed him
Even at the heels in golden multitudes.
He presently, as greatness knows itself,
Steps me a little higher than his vow   75
Made to my father, while his blood was poor,
Upon the naked shore at Ravenspurgh;
And now, forsooth, takes on him to reform
Some certain edicts and some strait decrees
That lie too heavy on the commonwealth;   80
Cries out upon abuses, seems to weep
Over his country's wrongs; and by this face,
This seeming brow of justice, did he win
The hearts of all that he did angle for;
Proceeded further—cut me off the heads   85
Of all the favorites that the absent King
In deputation left behind him here
When he was personal in the Irish war.

BLUNT.   Tut! I came not to hear this.

HOT   Then to the point.
In short time after he depos'd the King;   90
Soon after that depriv'd him of his life;
And in the neck of that task'd the whole state;
To make that worse, suff'red his kinsman March
(Who is, if every owner were well plac'd,
Indeed his king) to be engag'd in Wales,   95
There without ransom to lie forfeited;

---

65. **perform'd it:** fulfilled his oath. 68. **The more and less:** the high and low.—**with cap and knee:** cap in hand and with bended knee. 70. **Attended him:** awaited his coming.—**in lanes:** in rows or lines, one on each side of the road. 73. **golden:** richly dressed. 74. **as greatness knows itself:** as his power gradually recognizes how great it has become. 76. **while his blood was poor:** while he was still poor in spirit—humble-minded. 78. **forsooth.** An ironical interjection. 79. **strait:** over-strict, and therefore oppressive. 81. **upon:** against. 82–83. **face:** pretence, pretext.—**seeming brow:** appearance, guise. 87–88. **In deputation:** in charge of the realm as his deputies.—**personal...war:** personally engaged in the war in Ireland. 92. **in the neck of that:** immediately after that. —**task'd:** taxed. 94. **were well plac'd:** had his rightful position in the state. 95. **engag'd:** pledged, i.e., as a hostage. 96. **to lie forfeited:** to be held prisoner (like a pawned article that has not been redeemed).

Disgrac'd me in my happy victories,
Sought to entrap me by intelligence;
Rated mine uncle from the Council board;
In rage dismiss'd my father from the court;   100
Broke oath on oath, committed wrong on wrong;
And in conclusion drove us to seek out
This head of safety, and withal to pry
Into his title, the which we find
Too indirect for long continuance. — *indirect from line of*   105
                                        succession

BLUNT.   Shall I return this answer to the King?

HOT.   Not so, Sir Walter. We'll withdraw awhile.
Go to the King; and let there be impawn'd
Some surety for a safe return again,
And in the morning early shall mine uncle   110
Bring him our purposes; and so farewell.

BLUNT.   I would you would accept of grace and love.

HOT.   And may be so we shall.

BLUNT.   Pray God you do.   *Exeunt.*

SCENE IV. [*York. The* Archbishop's *Palace.*]

Enter the Archbishop of York *and* Sir Michael.

ARCH.   Hie, good Sir Michael; bear this sealed brief
With winged haste to the Lord Marshal;
This to my cousin Scroop; and all the rest
To whom they are directed. If you knew
How much they do import, you would make haste.   5

SIR M.   My good lord,
I guess their tenor.

ARCH.   Like enough you do.

---

97. **Disgrac'd…victories:** made my victories the means of disgracing me. 98. **by intelligence:** by means of spies. 99. **Rated:** berated; scolded; expelled with contumely. 103–105. **this head of safety:** this armed troop, mustered to protect us. Hotspur plays with the word *head,* which means also "source."—**withal:** at the same time.—**his title:** i.e., to the crown.—**Too indirect:** too irregular—literally, too far from the direct line of succession. 108. **impawn'd:** left as a pledge or surety. Westmoreland was thus impawned. 109–110. **a safe return:** i.e., my uncle's safe return.—**mine uncle:** the Earl of Worcester. 111. **our purposes:** our proposals, our terms. 112. **grace:** pardon and favor from the King.
SCENE IV
This scene takes place, presumably, at the Archbishop of York's palace. 1. **Sir Michael.** Unknown to history. Doubtless a priest in the service of the Archbishop. *Sir (Dominus)* was a priest's title.—**brief:** letter. 4. **To whom:** to those to whom. 5. **How…import:** how important they are. 7. **tenor:** purport.

Tomorrow, good Sir Michael, is a day
Wherein the fortune of ten thousand men
Must bide the touch; for, sir, at Shrewsbury,   10
As I am truly given to understand,
The King with mighty and quick-raised power
Meets with Lord Harry; and I fear, Sir Michael,
What with the sickness of Northumberland,
Whose power was in the first proportion,   15
And what with Owen Glendower's absence thence,
Who with them was a rated sinew too
And comes not in, overrul'd by prophecies—
I fear the power of Percy is too weak
To wage an instant trial with the King.   20

SIR M.   Why, my good lord, you need not fear;
There is Douglas and Lord Mortimer.

ARCH.   No, Mortimer is not there.

SIR M.   But there is Mordake, Vernon, Lord Harry Percy,
And there is my Lord of Worcester, and a head   25
Of gallant warriors, noble gentlemen.

ARCH.   And so there is; but yet the King hath drawn
The special head of all the land together—
The Prince of Wales, Lord John of Lancaster,
The noble Westmoreland and warlike Blunt,   30
And many moe corrivals and dear men
Of estimation and command in arms.

SIR M.   I doubt not, my lord, they shall be well oppos'd.

ARCH.   I hope no less, yet needful 'tis to fear;
And, to prevent the worst, Sir Michael, speed.   35
For if Lord Percy thrive not, ere the King
Dismiss his power, he means to visit us,
For he hath heard of our confederacy,
And 'tis but wisdom to make strong against him.
Therefore make haste. I must go write again   40
To other friends; and so farewell, Sir Michael.   *Exeunt.*

---

10. **bide the touch:** stand the test. A figure from the use of the touchstone to test gold. 15. **in the first proportion:** larger than any of the other troops. 17. **a rated sinew:** a support on which they counted. 20. **wage:** risk. 22. **Mortimer.** With the absence of Northumberland, Glendower, and Mortimer Hotspur's forces are seriously depleted. A more prudent general might have delayed a confrontation with the king at this moment. [s.c.] 25. **head:** armed troop. 31–32. **moe:** more.—**corrivals:** associates, comrades.—**dear men Of estimation…arms:** men who are highly valued as experienced generals. 35. **prevent:** forestall; hinder by precautionary measures. 37. **visit:** come against.

ACT V

SCENE I. [*The* King's *camp near Shrewsbury.*]

Enter the King, Prince of Wales, Lord John of Lancaster, Sir Walter Blunt, Falstaff.

KING.   How bloodily the sun begins to peer
          Above yon busky hill! The day looks pale
          At his distemp'rature.

PRINCE.   The southern wind
          Doth play the trumpet to his purposes
          And by his hollow whistling in the leaves   5
          Foretells a tempest and a blust'ring day.

KING.   Then with the losers let it sympathize,
          For nothing can seem foul to those that win.

          The trumpet sounds. Enter Worcester [*and* Vernon].

          How now, my Lord of Worcester? 'Tis not well
          That you and I should meet upon such terms   10
          As now we meet. You have deceiv'd our trust
          And made us doff our easy robes of peace
          To crush our old limbs in ungentle steel.
          This is not well, my lord; this is not well.
          What say you to it? Will you again unknit   15
          This churlish knot of all-abhorred war,
          And move in that obedient orb again
          Where you did give a fair and natural light,
          And be no more an exhal'd meteor,
          A prodigy of fear, and a portent   20
          Of broached mischief to the unborn times?

WOR.   Hear me, my liege.
          For mine own part, I could be well content

ACT V. SCENE I.
The king's camp at Shrewsbury. 1–3. **How bloodily,** etc. A red sun at dawn is a traditional sign of stormy weather. An old rhyme, still current, runs thus: Red sky in the morning, Sailors take warning; Red sky at night, Sailors' delight. —**busky:** bushy, wooded.—**pale At his distemp'rature:** as if terrified by the sun's disorder, i.e., unnatural (literally, unhealthy) appearance. 4. **trumpet:** trumpeter.—**his purposes:** acts like a trumpeter announcing what the sun portends. [s.c.] 7–8. **sympathize:** agree; be in accord.—**foul:** bad weather. 15–16. **again unknit...war:** untangle the disorder in which war (hated by all) has involved the realm. 17. **that obedient orb:** that sphere—loyal obedience—which should naturally regulate your actions. The metaphor is derived from the old astronomy. The earth was the centre of the universe. The planets were fixed in hollow spheres concentric with the earth. 20–21. **A prodigy of fear:** a terrifying omen of evil.—**a portént:** an ominous sign.—**Of broached mischief... times:** of harm now let loose and destined to bring disaster to future generations. To *broach* is, literally, to "tap" a cask of some liquid.

	To entertain the lag-end of my life	
	With quiet hours; for I do protest	25
	I have not sought the day of this dislike.	
KING.	You have not sought it! How comes it then?	
FAL.	Rebellion lay in his way, and he found it.	
PRINCE.	Peace, chewet, peace!	
WOR.	It pleas'd your Majesty to turn your looks	30
	Of favor from myself and all our house;	
	And yet I must remember you, my lord,	
	We were the first and dearest of your friends.	
	For you my staff of office did I break	
	In Richard's time, and posted day and night	35
	To meet you on the way and kiss your hand	
	When yet you were in place and in account	
	Nothing so strong and fortunate as I.	
	It was myself, my brother, and his son	
	That brought you home and boldly did outdare	40
	The dangers of the time. You swore to us,	
	And you did swear that oath at Doncaster,	
	That you did nothing purpose 'gainst the state,	
	Nor claim no further than your new-fall'n right,	
	The seat of Gaunt, dukedom of Lancaster.	45
	To this we swore our aid. But in short space	
	It rain'd down fortune show'ring on your head,	
	And such a flood of greatness fell on you	
	What with our help, what with the absent King,	
	What with the injuries of a wanton time,	50
	The seeming sufferances that you had borne,	
	And the contrarious winds that held the King	
	So long in his unlucky Irish wars	
	That all in England did repute him dead—	
	And from this swarm of fair advantages	55
	You took occasion to be quickly woo'd	
	To gripe the general sway into your hand;	
	Forgot your oath to us at Doncaster;	
	And, being fed by us, you us'd us so	

24–26. **entertain:** pass.—**the day of this dislike:** this time of enmity. 29. **chewet:** jackdaw or chatterbox. [S.C.] 32. **remember:** remind. 34. **my staff...break.** Worcester, Holinshed records, being "lord steward of the kings house,...brake his white staffe (which is the representing signe and token of his office) and without delaie went to duke Henrie." 35. **posted:** rode posthaste. 38. **nothing:** by no means; not at all. 44–45. **new-fall'n:** that had recently fallen to your lot. 49. **the absent King:** the absence of King Richard. 50. **the injuries...time:** the abuses incident to a time of misgovernment. 56–57. **occasion:** the opportunity.—**general:** i.e., of the whole kingdom, not merely of your own dukedom.

As that ungentle gull, the cuckoo's bird, <u>lay eggs in others' nests</u>60
Useth the sparrow—did oppress our nest;
Grew by our feeding to so great a bulk
That even our love durst not come near your sight
For fear of swallowing; but with nimble wing
We were enforc'd for safety sake to fly   65
Out of your sight and raise this present head;
Whereby we stand opposed by such means
As you yourself have forg'd against yourself
By unkind usage, dangerous countenance,
And violation of all faith and troth   70
Sworn to us in your younger enterprise.

KING.   These things, indeed, you have articulate,
Proclaim'd at market crosses, read in churches,
To face the garment of rebellion
With some fine color that may please the eye   75
Of fickle changelings and poor discontents,
Which gape and rub the elbow at the news
Of hurlyburly innovation.
And never yet did insurrection want
Such water colors to impaint his cause,   80
Nor moody beggars, starving for a time
Of pell-mell havoc and confusion.

PRINCE.   In both our armies there is many a soul   *sees him as a worthy*
Shall pay full dearly for this encounter,   *threat — which allows*
If once they join in trial. Tell your nephew   *him to win before* 85
The Prince of Wales doth join with all the world *acknowledges him*
In praise of Henry Percy. By my hopes,
This present enterprise set off his head,   *element of sarcasm as well*
I do not think a braver gentleman,   *+self-serving: saying he is*
More active-valiant or more valiant-young, *honorable so that when*90
                                    he defeats him it is a bigger deal-prove
                                               himself

---

60. **ungentle gull:** rude nestling.—**bird:** young, offspring. 61. **the sparrow:** in whose nest the young cuckoo is hatched. The cuckoo lays its eggs in other birds' nests.—**did oppress our nest:** tyrannized over our whole nest. 63–64. **our love:** we who loved you. 66–69. **head…usage:** army, by means of which we now stand in opposition to you, induced by causes that you yourself have contrived against yourself by your unnatural treatment of us.—**dangerous countenance:** your threatening behaviour. 70. **troth:** one's pledged word. 71. **in…enterprise:** at the outset of your undertaking. 72–73. **articulate:** articulated; drawn up in formal shape, item by item.—**market crosses:** crosses that stand in the public squares of market towns. 74. **face:** trim, adorn. 76. **changelings:** fickle persons; turncoats.—**discontents:** malcontents. 77. **gape:** listen eagerly, open-mouthed. —**rub the elbow:** hug themselves (in delight), with arms crossed and each elbow in the palm of the other hand—or some similar gesture. 80–81. **water colors:** slight pretexts.—**moody:** sullen, discontented.—**beggars.** Object of the verb *did want.* 83. **both our armies:** i.e., both the King's and Percy's. 88. **This present enterprise…head:** if we strike this present enterprise (the rebellion) off his account—disregard it in our judgment of him. 89. **braver:** nobler. A general term of commendation for fine qualities—not restricted to valor.

More daring or more bold, is now alive
To grace this latter age with noble deeds.
For my part, I may speak it to my shame,
I have a truant been to chivalry;
And so I hear he doth account me too.   95
Yet this before my father's Majesty—
I am content that he shall take the odds
Of his great name and estimation,
And will, to save the blood on either side,
Try fortune with him in a single fight.   100

KING.   And, Prince of Wales, so dare we venture thee,
Albeit considerations infinite
Do make against it. No, good Worcester, no!
We love our people well; even those we love
That are misled upon your cousin's part;   105
And, will they take the offer of our grace,
Both he, and they, and you, yea, every man
Shall be my friend again, and I'll be his.
So tell your cousin, and bring me word
What he will do. But if he will not yield,   110
Rebuke and dread correction wait on us,
And they shall do their office. So be gone.
We will not now be troubled with reply.
We offer fair; take it advisedly.   *Exit Worcester [with Vernon].*

PRINCE.   It will not be accepted, on my life.   115
The Douglas and the Hotspur both together
Are confident against the world in arms.

KING.   Hence, therefore, every leader to his charge;
For, on their answer, will we set on them,
And God befriend us as our cause is just!   120
                         Exeunt. Manent Prince, Falstaff.

FAL.   Hal, if thou see me down in the battle and bestride me, so! 'Tis a point
of friendship.

PRINCE.   Nothing but a Colossus can do thee that friendship. Say thy prayers,
and farewell.

---

95. **account:** regard, think. 98. **estimation:** reputation. 101. **we.** The "royal *we.*"102. **Albeit:** although.
105. **upon...part:** by taking sides with your kinsman—Percy. 106. **grace:** pardon and favor. 111. **wait
on us:** are my attendants; are ready to act at a word from me. 114. **take it advisedly:** consider my offer
carefully. 118. **charge:** his division or troop. 119. **on their answer:** as soon as they have answered. The
King agrees with the Prince in expecting a refusal. 121. **bestride me:** i.e., in order to defend me.—**so!** well
and good! 123. **a Colossus.** The Colossus of Rhodes, one of the wonders of the ancient world, was a huge
statue dedicated to the sun. It stood near the harbor; and the current belief in Shakespeare's time was that it
bestrode the entrance of the harbor, so that ships sailed between its legs.

Falstaff (Anthony Quayle) delivering his disquisition on "honor." (BBC-TV)

FAL.   I would 'twere bedtime, Hal, and all well.   125

PRINCE.   Why, thou owest God a death.   [*Exit.*]

FAL.   'Tis not due yet. I would be loath to pay him before his day. What need I
            be so forward with him that calls not on me? Well, 'tis no matter; honor
            pricks me on. Yea, but how if honor prick me off when I come on? How
            then? Can honor set to a leg? No. Or an arm? No. Or take away the
            grief of a wound? No. Honor hath no skill in surgery then? No. What is
            honor? A word. What is that word honor? Air. A trim reckoning! Who
            hath it? He that died a Wednesday. Doth he feel it? No. Doth he hear it?
            No. 'Tis insensible then? Yea, to the dead. But will it not live with the
            living? No. Why? Detraction will not suffer it. Therefore I'll none of it.
            Honor is a mere scutcheon—and so ends my catechism.   *Exit.*

126. **owest God a death.** With a pun on "debt" as "debt" and "death" were similarly pronounced in
Shakespeare's age. [S.C.] 129. **pricks:** spurs.—**prick me off:** check my name off the list (of living men). To
prick a name in a list was to mark it with a puncture or dot. 130–131. **Can honor,** etc. Here Falstaff begins
to speak in the tone and manner of a person catechizing (questioning closely) a boy; and, in the answers,
he imitates the boy who speaks mechanically, having learned them by heart.—**set to a leg:** set a broken
leg or attach a leg that has been cut off. The accent is on *to.*—**grief:** pain. 132–133. **A trim reckoning!** A
fine sum total! This ironical comment interrupts the steady course of the "catechism."—**a Wednesday:**
on Wednesday; last Wednesday. 134. **insensible:** not perceptible by the senses. 135. **Detraction:** slander.
—**suffer:** allow. 136. **I'll none of it:** I'll have nothing to do with it. 137. **scutcheon:** hatchment—a
funeral tablet, with coat of arms and mourning emblems, set up on a tomb or a house-front, or over a gate.
For Falstaff honor is nothing more than a cheap piece of heraldry to be displayed at funerals. [S.C.]—**so
ends my catechism.** Those critics who take Falstaff's "catechism" as a serious confession of faith, and
therefore as proof of cowardice, lack a sense of humor. What it expresses is the half-cynical mood of a
veteran soldier who has outlived the romance of warfare. The contrast with the Prince's untried eagerness
for single combat with Percy and Percy's determination to fight against the odds is complete.

SCENE II. [*The rebel camp.*]

Enter Worcester *and* Sir Richard Vernon.

WOR. O no, my nephew must not know, Sir Richard,
      The liberal and kind offer of the King.

VER. 'Twere best he did.

WOR.   Then are we all undone.
      It is not possible, it cannot be,
      The King should keep his word in loving us.   5
      He will suspect us still and find a time
      To punish this offence in other faults.
      Suspicion all our lives shall be stuck full of eyes;
      For treason is but trusted like the fox,
      Who, ne'er so tame, so cherish'd and lock'd up,   10
      Will have a wild trick of his ancestors.
      Look how we can, or sad or merrily,
      Interpretation will misquote our looks,
      And we shall feed like oxen at a stall,
      The better cherish'd, still the nearer death.   15
      My nephew's trespass may be well forgot;
      It hath the excuse of youth and heat of blood,
      And an adopted name of privilege—
      A hare-brain'd Hotspur, govern'd by a spleen.
      All his offences live upon my head   20
      And on his father's. We did train him on;
      And, his corruption being ta'en from us,
      We, as the spring of all, shall pay for all.
      Therefore, good cousin, let not Harry know,
      In any case, the offer of the King.   25

                    Enter Hotspur [*and* Douglas].

VER. Deliver what you will, I'll say 'tis so.
      Here comes your cousin.

SCENE II
The rebel camp. 3. **undone:** ruined. 6–7. **suspect us still:** always be suspicious of us.—**in:** in punishing. 10–11. **ne'er so tame:** be he ever so tame; no matter how tame he is.—**trick:** trait. 12. **sad:** serious.—**merrily:** cheerful. 13. **Interpretation:** i.e., on the King's part. 18. **And...privilege:** and his fault has the additional excuse, in men's eyes, of having been committed by one who goes by a nickname that gives a kind of authorization for any wild actions. 19. **a spleen:** mere whim and impulse. 20. **his offences... head:** his offences against the King may be forgotten and forgiven so far as Hotspur himself is concerned, but they are still alive (in the King's memory) as acts for which *I* am held accountable. 21. **We...on:** We (it will be said) enticed him to take part in the rebellion. 22–23. **his corruption:** his guilt.—**spring:** source. 25. **In any case:** on any consideration; whatever the result may be. 26. **Deliver:** report.

HOT.	My uncle is return'd.	
	Deliver up my Lord of Westmoreland.	
	Uncle, what news?	
WOR.	The King will bid you battle presently.	30
DOUG.	Defy him by the Lord of Westmoreland.	
HOT.	Lord Douglas, go you and tell him so.	
DOUG.	Marry, and shall, and very willingly.	*Exit.*
WOR.	There is no seeming mercy in the King.	
HOT.	Did you beg any? God forbid!	35
WOR.	I told him gently of our grievances,	
	Of his oath-breaking; which he mended thus,	
	By now forswearing that he is forsworn.	
	He calls us rebels, traitors, and will scourge	
	With haughty arms this hateful name in us.	40

Enter Douglas.

DOUG.	Arm, gentlemen! to arms! for I have thrown	
	A brave defiance in King Henry's teeth,	
	And Westmoreland, that was engag'd, did bear it;	
	Which cannot choose but bring him quickly on.	
WOR.	The Prince of Wales stepp'd forth before the King	45
	And, nephew, challeng'd you to single fight.	
HOT.	O, would the quarrel lay upon our heads,	
	And that no man might draw short breath today	
	But I and Harry Monmouth! Tell me, tell me,	
	How show'd his tasking? Seem'd it in contempt?	50
VER.	No, by my soul. I never in my life	
	Did hear a challenge urg'd more modestly,	
	Unless a brother should a brother dare	
	To gentle exercise and proof of arms.	
	He gave you all the duties of a man;	55

---

28. **Deliver up:** release. 30. **bid:** offer.—**presently:** at once. 33. **Marry, and shall:** Indeed I will. 34. **no seeming mercy:** nothing that looks like mercy. 37–38. **mended:** amended, made up for.—**By...forsworn:** by now taking a false oath that he did not violate his former oath. 39–40. **will...in us:** he is determined (so he says) to scourge us as rebels and traitors. 43. **engag'd:** held as a hostage for the safe return of Worcester and Vernon from their interview with the King. 47. **the quarrel:** the whole cause (for which we fight). 48. **draw short breath:** i.e., in fight. 50. **show'd:** appeared.—**his tasking:** his challenge. To *task or tax* is, literally, to "take one to task," to "call one to account." 52. **urg'd:** offered or proposed. To *urge* often means merely to "propose," "suggest," "mention," without the implication of urgency or special emphasis. 54. **proof of arms:** test of skill in combat. 55. **gave...man:** he gave you all the dues of a man—all the praise that is due to manly qualities.

Trimm'd up your praises with a princely tongue;
Spoke your deservings like a chronicle;
Making you ever better than his praise
By still dispraising praise valued with you;
And, which became him like a prince indeed,   60
He made a blushing cital of himself,
And chid his truant youth with such a grace
As if he mast'red there a double spirit
Of teaching and of learning instantly.
There did he pause; but let me tell the world,   65
If he outlive the envy of this day,
England did never owe so sweet a hope,
So much misconstrued in his wantonness.

HOT.   Cousin, I think thou art enamoured
Upon his follies. Never did I hear   70
Of any prince so wild a libertine.
But be he as he will, yet once ere night
I will embrace him with a soldier's arm,
That he shall shrink under my courtesy.
Arm, arm with speed! and, fellows, soldiers, friends,   75
Better consider what you have to do
Than I, that have not well the gift of tongue,
Can lift your blood up with persuasion.

Enter a Messenger.

MESS.   My lord, here are letters for you.

I ᴘᴇʀ   I cannot read them now.—   80
O gentlemen, the time of life is short!
To spend that shortness basely were too long
If life did ride upon a dial's point,
Still ending at the arrival of an hour.
An if we live, we live to tread on kings;   85
If die, brave death, when princes die with us!
Now for our consciences, the arms are fair,
When the intent of bearing them is just.

Enter another Messenger.

---

59. **By…with you:** by always insisting that no praise, however great, could do you justice. 61. **cital:** mention. 63–64. **mast'red there…instantly:** were master, on that occasion, of the power to teach and readiness to learn—both at the same moment. 66–67. **envy:** malice, malignity.—**owe:** own, possess. 68. **in his wantonness:** in the time of his sportive youth. 71. **libertine:** a "loose liver" in general. 74. **That:** so that. 75. **fellows:** comrades. 76 ff. **Better…persuasion:** Consider what you have to accomplish in this battle, and that thought will rouse your courage better than any exhortation from me, for I am no orator. 84. **Still:** always, i.e., in the case of every man—if no man's life were longer than an hour. 86. **brave:** glorious. 87. **for:** as for.—**fair:** just, righteous.

MESS.   My lord, prepare. The King comes on apace.

HOT.   I thank him that he cuts me from my tale,   90
        For I profess not talking. Only this—
        Let each man do his best; and here draw I
        A sword whose temper I intend to stain
        With the best blood that I can meet withal
        In the adventure of this perilous day.   95
        Now, Esperance! Percy! and set on.
        Sound all the lofty instruments of war,
        And by that music let us all embrace;
        For, heaven to earth, some of us never shall
        A second time do such a courtesy.   100
        Here they embrace. The trumpets sound.   [*Exeunt.*]

SCENE III. [*Plain between the camps.*]

The King *enters with his* Power. *Alarum to the battle.*
Then enter Douglas *and* Sir Walter Blunt.

BLUNT. What is thy name, that in the battle thus
        Thou crossest me? What honor dost thou seek
        Upon my head?

DOUG.   Know then my name is Douglas,
        And I do haunt thee in the battle thus
        Because some tell me that thou art a king.   5

BLUNT. They tell thee true.

DOUG.   The Lord of Stafford dear today hath bought
        Thy likeness; for instead of thee, King Harry,
        This sword hath ended him. So shall it thee,
        Unless thou yield thee as my prisoner.   10

BLUNT. I was not born a yielder, thou proud Scot;
        And thou shalt find a king that will revenge
        Lord Stafford's death.
                            They fight. Douglas kills Blunt.
                    Then enter Hotspur.

94–95. **withal:** with.—**the adventure:** the chances. 96. **Esperance! Percy!** The battle cry of the Percys.
99. **heaven to earth:** One might wager heaven to earth. The odds are infinity to nothing.
SCENE III
The battlefield at Shrewsbury. 1. (stage direction). **Alarum:** the trumpet signal to arms—(*all' arme*)—
to the onset. 2. **Thou crossest me:** You cross my path continually.

HOT.	O Douglas, hadst thou fought at Holmedon thus,
	I never had triumph'd upon a Scot. 15
DOUG.	All's done, all's won. Here breathless lies the King.
HOT.	Where?
DOUG.	Here.
HOT.	This, Douglas? No. I know this face full well.
	A gallant knight he was, his name was Blunt; 20
	Semblably furnish'd like the King himself.
DOUG.	A fool go with thy soul, whither it goes!
	A borrowed title hast thou bought too dear:
	Why didst thou tell me that thou wert a king?
HOT.	The King hath many marching in his coats. 25
DOUG.	Now, by my sword, I will kill all his coats;
	I'll murder all his wardrobe, piece by piece,
	Until I meet the King.
HOT.	Up and away!
	Our soldiers stand full fairly for the day. *Exeunt.* 29

Alarum. Enter Falstaff *solus.*

FAL.   Though I could scape shot-free at London, I fear the shot here. Here's no scoring but upon the pate. Soft! who are you? Sir Walter Blunt. There's honor for you! Here's no vanity! I am as hot as molten lead, and as heavy too. God keep lead out of me! I need no more weight than mine own bowels. I have led my rag-of-muffins where they are pepper'd. There's not three of my hundred and fifty left alive; and they are for the town's end, to beg during life. But who comes here? 36

Enter the Prince.

PRINCE.   What, stand'st thou idle here? Lend me thy sword.
Many a nobleman lies stark and stiff
Under the hoofs of vaunting enemies,

---

21. **Semblably furnished like:** so armed and attired as to seem exactly like. 22. **A fool go with thy soul:** i.e., the epithet "fool." "Farewell to thy foolish soul!" A standard form of gibe at parting. —**whither:** whithersoever. 25. **in his coats:** i.e., with the royal coat of arms on the coat that covers the armor. Douglas puns on the word. 29. **fairly for the day:** in a way that bids fair to win the day. 30. **shot-free:** without paying the shot, i.e., the scot, the reckoning at taverns. *Shot* in this use is another form of *scot*. 31. **scoring.** A pun on *scoring*: (1) scoring up an account (literally, by cutting notches in a tally stick; then, by making chalk marks: see 2.4.21); (2) making cuts or slashes (on one's body or head).—**Soft!** Wait a moment! 32. **Here's no vanity!** Here's a good example how vain (empty) a thing this *honor* is! 34. **rag-of-muffins.** An old form of *ragamuffins.* 36. **for the town's end:** only fit to haunt the places where the highway enters the town—in a walled city, the gates. Vagabond beggars gathered there, to take advantage of the traffic.

Whose deaths are yet unreveng'd. I prithee   40
Lend me thy sword.

FAL.   O Hal, I prithee give me leave to breathe awhile. Turk Gregory never
did such deeds in arms as I have done this day. I have paid Percy; I
have made him sure.

PRINCE.   He is indeed, and living to kill thee.   45
I prithee lend me thy sword.

FAL.   Nay, before God, Hal, if Percy be alive, thou get'st not my sword; but
take my pistol, if thou wilt.

PRINCE.   Give it me. What, is it in the case?

FAL.   Ay, Hal. 'Tis hot, 'tis hot. There's that will sack a city.   50
The Prince draws it out and finds it to be a bottle of sack.

PRINCE.   What, is it a time to jest and dally now? *He throws the bottle at him.*

Exit.

FAL.   Well, if Percy be alive, I'll pierce him. If he do come in my way, so; if
he do not, if I come in his willingly, let him make a carbonado of me. I
like not such grinning honor as Sir Walter hath. Give me life; which if
I can save, so; if not, honor comes unlook'd for, and there's an end.

Exit.

SCENE IV. [*Another part of the field.*]

Alarum. Excursions. Enter the King, *the* Prince, Lord John of Lancaster,
Earl of Westmoreland.

KING.   I prithee,
Harry, withdraw thyself; thou bleedest too much.
Lord John of Lancaster, go you with him.

JOHN.   Not I, my lord, unless I did bleed too.

PRINCE.   I do beseech your Majesty make up,   5
Lest your retirement do amaze your friends.

---

40. **unreveng'd:** unavenged. 42. **Turk Gregory.** Apparently Falstaff refers to Pope Gregory VII (Hilde-brand), of whom wild stories were told. *Turk* implies ferocious belligerency. 43–44. **paid Percy:** given him his payment; settled his account.—**I have made him sure:** I have made sure of him. 45. **He is indeed:** He is indeed *sure*—safe and sound. The Prince puns on *sure.* 51. **dally:** waste time in trifling. 52. **pierce.** Pronounced *perce.*—**so:** well and good. 53. **a carbonado:** a piece of meat cut crosswise and grilled. [s.c.] 55. **there's an end:** that's the conclusion of the whole matter; that winds up the subject.
SCENE IV
Another part of the battlefield. 5–6. **make up:** advance.—**amaze:** confound; disconcert.

KING.   I will do so.
             My Lord of Westmoreland, lead him to his tent.

WEST.   Come, my lord, I'll lead you to your tent.

PRINCE.   Lead me, my lord? I do not need your help;   10
             And God forbid a shallow scratch should drive
             The Prince of Wales from such a field as this,
             Where stain'd nobility lies trodden on,
             And rebels' arms triumph in massacres!

JOHN.   We breathe too long. Come, cousin Westmoreland,   15
             Our duty this way lies. For God's sake, come.
                              [*Exeunt Prince John and Westmoreland.*]

PRINCE.   By God, thou hast deceiv'd me, Lancaster!
             I did not think thee lord of such a spirit.
             Before, I lov'd thee as a brother, John;
             But now, I do respect thee as my soul.   20

KING.   I saw him hold Lord Percy at the point
             With lustier maintenance than I did look for
             Of such an ungrown warrior.

PRINCE.   O, this boy
             Lends mettle to us all!   *Exit.*

                              Enter Douglas.

DOUG.   Another king? They grow like Hydra's heads.   25
             I am the Douglas, fatal to all those
             That wear those colors on them. What art thou
             That counterfeit'st the person of a king?

KING.   The King himself, who, Douglas, grieves at heart
             So many of his shadows thou hast met,   30
             And not the very King. I have two boys
             Seek Percy and thyself about the field;
             But, seeing thou fall'st on me so luckily,
             I will assay thee. So defend thyself.

DOUG.   I fear thou art another counterfeit;   35
             And yet, in faith, thou bearest thee like a king.
             But mine I am sure thou art, whoe'er thou be,
             And thus I win thee.

---

15. **breathe:** pause to take breath. 20. **respect thee as:** hold thee in as high regard as. 21. **at the point:** at sword's points. 22. **lustier maintenance:** more vigorous action. 25. **Hydra's heads.** From Greek mythology; as fast as one of the Hydra's many heads was cut off, two heads grew in its place. 27. **those colors:** the colors in the King's coat of arms. 34. **assay:** make trial of.

They fight. The King *being in danger, enter* Prince of Wales.

PRINCE.   Hold up thy head, vile Scot, or thou art like
Never to hold it up again! The spirits   40
Of valiant Shirley, Stafford, Blunt are in my arms.
It is the Prince of Wales that threatens thee,
Who never promiseth but he means to pay.
They fight. Douglas flieth.
Cheerly, my lord. How fares your Grace?
Sir Nicholas Gawsey hath for succour sent,   45
And so hath Clifton. I'll to Clifton straight.

KING.   Stay and breathe awhile.
Thou hast redeem'd thy lost opinion,
And show'd thou mak'st some tender of my life,
In this fair rescue thou hast brought to me.   50

PRINCE.   O God! they did me too much injury
That ever said I heark'ned for your death.
If it were so, I might have let alone
The insulting hand of Douglas over you,
Which would have been as speedy in your end   55
As all the poisonous potions in the world,
And sav'd the treacherous labor of your son.

KING.   Make up to Clifton; I'll to Sir Nicholas Gawsey.   *Exit.*

Enter Hotspur.

HOT.   If I mistake not, thou art Harry Monmouth.

PRINCE.   Thou speak'st as if I would deny my name.   60

HOT.   My name is Harry Percy.

PRINCE.   Why, then I see
A very valiant rebel of the name.
I am the Prince of Wales; and think not, Percy,
To share with me in glory any more.
Two stars keep not their motion in one sphere,   65
Nor can one England brook a double reign
Of Harry Percy and the Prince of Wales.

---

39. **like:** likely. 44. **Cheerly.** Merely an encouraging exclamation. 48. **opinion:** reputation. 49. **mak'st some tender of my life:** holdest my life in some regard. 50. **rescue.** Holinshed reports: "The king... aduentured so farre, that (as some write) the earle Dowglas strake him downe, & at that instant slue Sir Walter Blunt, and three other, apparelled in the kings sute and clothing, saieng: 'I maruell to see so many kings thus suddenlie arise one in the necke of an other.' The king, indeed, was raised." But Holinshed does not tell who rescued him. 58. **Make up to:** Advance to. 65–66. **stars:** planets.—**brook:** endure.

HOT.	Nor shall it, Harry; for the hour is come
	To end the one of us; and would to God
	Thy name in arms were now as great as mine! 70
PRINCE.	I'll make it greater ere I part from thee,
	And all the budding honors on thy crest
	I'll crop to make a garland for my head.
HOT.	I can no longer brook thy vanities. *They fight.*[†]

Enter Falstaff.

FAL.	Well said, Hal! to it, Hal! Nay, you shall find no boy's play here, I can
	tell you. 76

Enter Douglas. *He fighteth with Falstaff, who falls down as if he were dead.*

[Exit Douglas.]

The Prince *killeth* Percy.

HOT.	O Harry, thou hast robb'd me of my youth!
	I better brook the loss of brittle life
	Than those proud titles thou hast won of me.
	They wound my thoughts worse than thy sword my flesh. 80
	But thoughts, the slaves of life, and life, time's fool,
	And time, that takes survey of all the world,
	Must have a stop. O, I could prophesy,
	But that the earthy and cold hand of death

---

75. **Well said:** Well done. With regard to the question whether Falstaff is a coward or not, we should note that he has been in the thick of the fight and that he makes his appearance (as here) in the most dangerous possible places. 79. **hast won.** Holinshed informs us that Hotspur was killed, but he does not say who killed him. 81–83. **But thoughts...stop:** But *thoughts* (which are absolutely dependent upon life) and *life* (which is subject to time) and even *time itself* (which measures all things earthly) must come to an end.—**time's fool.** As the fool is subjected to every whim of the other members of a household, so life is time's sport and fool for the length of one's life depends, as it were, on the mere whim of time.—**Must have a stop.** "And the angel...sware by him that liveth for ever and ever,...That there should be time no longer" (*Revelation,* x, 5, 6). 83. **prophesy.** It was an old idea that a dying man has some measure of prophetic power, since he looks, as it were, into the world to come.

---

† Directors are given great latitude in staging Shakespeare's fights. In Welles's version of the battle of Shrewsbury the two armies are practically indistinguishable as they slog through the rain and mud. The Hal-Hotspur duel is not presented as the epic clash between two vibrant heroes but as the confrontation of two exhausted, weary fighters who can barely muster the energy to lift their heavy swords. Hal (Keith Baxter) triumphs because he has an ounce or two more of energy at the end of a long fight than his rival. In the ESC version Hal's triumph is a bit more tarnished. At one moment in the fight Hotspur has unarmed him and Hal (Michael Pennington) kneels on the ground and trembles awaiting the death blow; but Hotspur (Andrew Jarvis) won't kill an unarmed man, so he slides Hal his sword and the two resume their encounter. Later when Hal has the advantage and has wounded Hotspur he does not return the favor but, after a pause, he plunges his sword back into his rival's body, making sure he is dead. [s.c.]

Lies on my tongue. No, Percy, thou art dust,   85
And food for—   [Dies.]‡
finishes the sentence – domination: one dies other rites
PRINCE.   For worms, brave Percy. Fare thee well, great heart!
Ill-weav'd ambition, how much art thou shrunk!
When that this body did contain a spirit,
A kingdom for it was too small a bound;   90
But now two paces of the vilest earth
Is room enough. This earth that bears thee dead
Bears not alive so stout a gentleman.
If thou wert sensible of courtesy,
I should not make so dear a show of zeal.   95
But let my favors hide thy mangled face;
And, even in thy behalf, I'll thank myself
For doing these fair rites of tenderness.
Adieu, and take thy praise with thee to heaven!
Thy ignominy sleep with thee in the grave,   100
But not rememb'red in thy epitaph!
                              He spieth Falstaff on the ground.
What, old acquaintance? Could not all this flesh
Keep in a little life? Poor Jack, farewell!
I could have better spar'd a better man.
O, I should have a heavy miss of thee   105
If I were much in love with vanity!
Death hath not struck so fat a deer today,
Though many dearer, in this bloody fray.
Embowell'd will I see thee by-and-by;
Till then in blood by noble Percy lie.   *Exit.* 110

                    Falstaff riseth up.

FAL.   Embowell'd? If thou embowel me today, I'll give you leave to powder
           me and eat me too tomorrow. 'Sblood, 'twas time to counterfeit, or

---

88. **Ill-weav'd.** Not meant of ambition in general, but only of such ambition as Hotspur's, which, the Prince thinks, was ill-conceived—unwarranted. 93. **stout:** brave, valiant. 95. **make so dear a show of zeal:** allow the warmth of my admiration to display itself so openly. 96. **favors:** a scarf or the like. So called because such things were worn as signs of a lady's favor. 97. **in thy behalf:** on thy part; as thy representative. 105. **I should have...of thee:** I should miss thee woefully (with a pun on the literal meaning of *heavy*). 106. **vanity:** the vain pursuits of life; frivolity. 109. **Embowell'd:** disembowelled (for embalming).—**by-and-by:** presently. 112. **to powder me:** to salt me down; to pickle me.

---

‡   Hotspur dies in mid-sentence and Hal picks up and finishes his thought (and iambic pentameter line) for him. Noting that Lady Percy refers to her husband as "speaking thick" in *Henry VI Part 2*, some actors have given their Hotspur a slight stammer. Most famously, Laurence Olivier gave him a stammer on the letter "w" so that his Hotspur died while trying to say "worms." [s.c.]

Falstaff (Barry Stanton) pulling out the "No Entry" sign he had used as a breastplate to save him from being killed by Douglas. (ESC-TV)

that hot termagant Scot had paid me scot and lot too. Counterfeit? I lie; I am no counterfeit. To die is to be a counterfeit; for he is but the counterfeit of a man who hath not the life of a man; but to counterfeit dying when a man thereby liveth, is to be no counterfeit, but the true and perfect image of life indeed. The better part of valor is discretion;* in the which better part I have saved my life. Zounds, I am afraid of this gunpowder Percy, though he be dead. How if he should counterfeit too, and rise? By my faith, I am afraid he would prove the better counterfeit. Therefore I'll make him sure; yea, and I'll swear I kill'd him. Why may not he rise as well as I? Nothing confutes me but eyes, and nobody sees me. Therefore, sirrah [*stabs him*], with a new wound in your thigh, come you along with me.

113, 114. **termagant:** raging. In the Middle Ages all Mohammedans were thought to be idolaters. One of their gods, it was believed, was *Termagant* (or *Tervagant*)—a ferocious demon. The origin of the name is unknown. —**paid me scot and lot too:** given me payment in full; settled accounts with me to the last item. *Scot and lot* was an old term for a kind of tax levied in proportion to one's means. *Scot* (without *lot*) was one's account at an inn—one's "hotel bill." 115. **the counterfeit of a man:** the imitation or picture of a man. 116. **thereby liveth:** saves his life by that means. 117–118. **The better part of valor is discretion.** *Part* is "quality"—not "portion": "Bravery that is not directed by good judgment is not true valor: it is mere foolhardiness." Such is the serious meaning of the maxim that Falstaff applies in witty defence of his stratagem. —**in:** in the exercise of. 122. **Why…I?** This foreshadows the story that Falstaff means to tell.

---

*   The Falstaff (Barry Stanton) in the ESC version got a huge laugh on this line by opening up his military tunic and producing a No Entry sign he had appropriated to use as a breast plate. [S.C.]

He takes up Hotspur on his back. Enter Prince, *and* John of Lancaster.

PRINCE.   Come, brother John; full bravely hast thou flesh'd   125
          Thy maiden sword.

JOHN.   But, soft! whom have we here?
          Did you not tell me this fat man was dead?

PRINCE.   I did; I saw him dead,
          Breathless and bleeding on the ground. Art thou alive,
          Or is it fantasy that plays upon our eyesight?   130
          I prithee speak. We will not trust our eyes
          Without our ears. Thou art not what thou seem'st.

FAL.   No, that's certain! I am not a double man; but if I be not Jack Falstaff,
          then am I a Jack. There is Percy. If your father will do me any honor,
          so; if not, let him kill the next Percy himself. I look to be either earl or
          duke, I can assure you.   136

PRINCE.   Why, Percy I kill'd myself, and saw thee dead!

FAL.   Didst thou? Lord, Lord, how this world is given to lying! I grant you
          I was down, and out of breath, and so was he; but we rose both at
          an instant and fought a long hour by Shrewsbury clock. If I may be
          believ'd, so; if not, let them that should reward valor bear the sin upon
          their own heads. I'll take it upon my death, I gave him this wound in
          the thigh. If the man were alive and would deny it, zounds!
          I would make him eat a piece of my sword.

JOHN.   This is the strangest tale that ever I heard.   145

PRINCE.   This is the strangest fellow, brother John.
          Come, bring your luggage nobly on your back.
          For my part, if a lie may do thee grace,
          I'll gild it with the happiest terms I have.**

                        A retreat is sounded.

---

125. **bravely:** nobly. —**flesh'd:** initiated. To *flesh* often means to "give one the first taste." 130. **fantasy:** imagination. 134. **a Jack:** a low rascal. 135. **so:** well and good. 141–142. **the sin:** i.e., the sin of discrediting my report and so refusing me my just reward.—**take it upon my death:** swear with death as the penalty for perjury. 148–149. **a lie:** i.e., a lie of yours.—**may do thee grace:** can win thee any favor.—**gild it:** ornament thy lie.—**happiest:** most felicitous; finest.

**   It is always interesting to see how the actor playing Hal treats this occasion when he has been
       embarrassed at a critical moment by Falstaff. Hal (David Gwillim) in the BBC version delivers
       the lines with a wide grin indicating that he accepts that Falstaff has managed to one-up him
       much as he had earlier turned the tables on Falstaff at the Gad's Hill robbery. In keeping with
       his more emotionally tortured performance throughout, the ESC Hal (Michael Pennington) is
       clearly angered by Falstaff's claim and chagrined that the fat knight has sought to throw doubt
       upon his victory over Hotspur. [s.c.]

The trumpet sounds retreat; the day is ours.   150
Come, brother, let's to the highest of the field,
To see what friends are living, who are dead.
                    Exeunt [Prince Henry and Prince John].

FAL.   I'll follow, as they say, for reward. He that rewards me, God reward
        him! If I do grow great, I'll grow less; for I'll purge, and leave sack, and
        live cleanly, as a nobleman should do.   *Exit [bearing off the body].*

SCENE V. [*Another part of the field.*]

The trumpets sound. Enter the King, Prince of Wales, Lord John of Lancaster, Earl of
        Westmoreland, *with* Worcester *and* Vernon *prisoners.*

KING.   Thus ever did rebellion find rebuke.
        Ill-spirited Worcester! did not we send grace,
        Pardon, and terms of love to all of you?
        And wouldst thou turn our offers contrary?
        Misuse the tenor of thy kinsman's trust?   5
        Three knights upon our party slain today,
        A noble earl, and many a creature else
        Had been alive this hour,
        If like a Christian thou hadst truly borne
        Betwixt our armies true intelligence.   10

WOR.   What I have done my safety urg'd me to;
        And I embrace this fortune patiently,
        Since not to be avoided it falls on me.

KING.   Bear Worcester to the death, and Vernon too;
        Other offenders we will pause upon.   15
                    Exeunt Worcester and Vernon, [guarded].
        How goes the field?

PRINCE. The noble Scot, Lord Douglas, when he saw
        The fortune of the day quite turn'd from him,
        The noble Percy slain, and all his men
        Upon the foot of fear, fled with the rest;   20

---

150. **sounds retreat:** gives notice to cease pursuing the enemy. 151. **the highest of the field:** the high ground, from which the whole field of battle could be seen. 153. **follow...for reward.** There is a slight pun on *follow* in the sense of "be one's follower."—**for reward:** rather than for loyal devotion. Falstaff here pays Hal back for stealing his prize at Gad's Hill. 154. **purge:** take cleansing medicines.
SCENE V
The scene continues and the play concludes at Shrewsbury. 2–3. **Ill-spirited:** evil-minded.—**we.** The royal *we.*—**grace:** promise of favor.—**terms of love:** loving words. 5. **Misuse...trust:** pervert the nature of the duty entrusted to thee by Harry Percy. 10. **intelligence:** information. 12. **patiently:** calmly. 15. **pause upon:** postpone consideration of. 20. **Upon the foot of fear:** fleeing in a panic.

And falling from a hill, he was so bruis'd
That the pursuers took him. At my tent
The Douglas is, and I beseech your Grace
I may dispose of him.

KING.   With all my heart.

PRINCE.   Then, brother John of Lancaster, to you   25
This honorable bounty shall belong.
Go to the Douglas and deliver him
Up to his pleasure, ransomless and free.
His valor shown upon our crests today
Hath taught us how to cherish such high deeds,   30
Even in the bosom of our adversaries.

JOHN.   I thank your Grace for this high courtesy,
Which I shall give away immediately.

KING.   Then this remains, that we divide our power.
You, son John, and my cousin Westmoreland,   35
Towards York shall bend you with your dearest speed
To meet Northumberland and the prelate Scroop,
Who, as we hear, are busily in arms.
Myself and you, son Harry, will towards Wales
To fight with Glendower and the Earl of March.   40
Rebellion in this land shall lose his sway,
Meeting the check of such another day;
And since this business so fair is done,
Let us not leave till all our own be won.   *Exeunt.*

---

24. **dispose of him:** have the disposal of him. 26. **This honorable bounty:** the honor of this gracious act. 33. **give away:** i.e., by passing it on—conferring it on Douglas. 34. **power:** army. 36. **bend you:** direct your course.—**dearest.** urgent. 37. **meet:** i.e., in a hostile encounter.—**Scroop:** Richard Scroop, the Archbishop of York. 40. **the Earl of March.** Mortimer. 41–42. **his:** its.—**Meeting the check:** if it meets with the hindrance. *Check* also suggests "rebuke"—a sense which it often bears. 43. **fair:** successfully.

HOW TO READ *THE FIRST PART OF KING HENRY THE FOURTH* AS PERFORMANCE

Shakespeare wrote scripts for performance rather than texts intended for publication. The success of those scripts when realized in production at the Theatre or the Globe is what led to the commercial demand that they be published so that they could be consumed and experienced on the page as well as the stage.

In our age, most of us first experience Shakespeare on the page rather than on the stage and we are taught to respond to his work as that of a great theater poet in full command of both his form and content. When reading Shakespeare we first become aware of the central characters in any given play and the basic narrative outline of the plot. We then learn to pluck out the major themes of the work, the complex clusters of images through which he expresses those themes, and the confident manner in which he structures the interaction of character, theme, and image. At a more advanced level we learn to read Shakespeare through a variety of intellectual approaches that speak powerfully to a given social moment. In recent decades those approaches have included (but have not been limited to) ego psychology, gender studies, cultural materialism, new historicism, and performance.

But when we read, we also imagine. We begin to project the characters and the action on the screen in our mind. Shakespeare does not give us, as many modern playwrights do, elaborate stage directions and descriptions of the set and the physical characteristics of his characters. His plays were conceived for an open stage with little or no representational scenery. That is why he can cut from one locale or landscape to another (from the court at Westminster to the tavern in Eastcheap and then from the tavern to the rebel camp in Wales) with the speed of modern film. Likewise he doesn't describe his characters, he dramatizes them. We learn about his characters from how they talk, what preoccupies their thoughts, what others say about them, and how they interact with one another.

For instance, in the very first lines of the play we learn that the king and the country are burdened by the civil turmoil he has created in overthrowing the previous king (Richard II): "So shaken as we are, so wan with care." And by the end of the scene we know that he is equally troubled by his son and heir, Prince Hal: "I...See...riot and dishonor stain the brow/Of my young Harry." Shakespeare

109

quickly establishes that Henry IV is confronted by challenges to his rule and legacy from external forces (the Welsh and Scots), from his former friends (the Percys), and from his own family (Prince Hal). The king is a man in crisis and that needs to be projected by the actor's posture and demeanor.

In the next scene we meet the king's opposite: Falstaff. Falstaff, unlike Henry IV, is carefree and has never met a crisis he couldn't exploit. His mission is to enjoy life and to wonder how the next drink and meal are to be paid for. The king's language is serious and straightforward as he confronts the challenges to his leadership. Falstaff's language is playful and witty and meant to convey subversive pleasure in his banter with the Prince. Because everyone—including himself—jokes about Falstaff's age and belly we quickly realize that he is large and round and old. Hotspur, as his name implies, is explosive and rash and young. He's a hothead, but an attractive one as Shakespeare demonstrates in the wonderful scene with his wife Kate as she tries to discover what momentous events are stirring in his dreams. Hotspur is a character fashioned in the traditional heroic mold.

Slowly, from the interaction of the characters in the text, we begin to build mental pictures not only of what the play's characters look like but what constitutes their psychological make-up as well. We also begin to discover that Shakespeare associates each of the principal characters (King Henry IV, Falstaff, and Hotspur) with a specific landscape: the court for the king; the tavern for Falstaff; and the rebel camp for Hotspur. The king is trapped in the corridors of power; Falstaff reigns over the world of play and pleasure; and Hotspur has become the outsider challenging the king for seizing the crown and his son for being a "madcap Prince of Wales."

Ideally, a production of the play should make us see the resonance between character and landscape. For instance, Orson Welles's film of the Hal-Falstaff material, *Chimes at Midnight,* repeatedly shoots the king (John Gielgud) against the cold, grey stone of the ancient Spanish cathedral that serves as the setting for the court scenes, while Falstaff is most often framed by the film against the wooden beams of the old barn that functions as the tavern, and Hotspur is often shot against the open sky indicating the boundless aspiration of his ambition. Lively readers begin to create their own movie versions of the play as they fully engage with the text. When those readers are then confronted with a production of the play, on stage or film or television, they need to see how well the director, designer, and actors have picked up crucial ideas from the text to inform movement, setting, and the creation of character.

Thinking about the play in performance also focuses on how the actors express the text at critical moments in the action. *1 Henry IV* provides several such moments including Hal's only soliloquy, his promise to banish Falstaff in the "play extempore," and his confrontation with his father in 3.2. Hal's soliloquy comes early in the narrative, at the end of the play's second scene. It is troublesome for many readers as it seems to present us with someone who is cold and calculating, thus undercutting the witty and fun-loving figure we have just seen bantering and trading insults with Falstaff. When observing a performance one needs to be alert to the way in which the actor playing Hal tries to work with this seeming contradiction in the delivery of the soliloquy. Does the actor treat the speech as a form of "thinking aloud" where he stumbles upon his strategy for reformation as he works through his predicament? Does he pace about as though he is lost in thought, pausing only when he comes to a formulation ("If all the year were playing holidays,/To sport would be as tedious as to work" for instance) that strikes him as particularly apt. Or does he deliver the speech directly at the audience with a Machiavellian sense of self-confidence that says: I know exactly what I'm doing; just watch me. Or does he use a prop, perhaps a pint of ale, to effect as an indication of how he plans "to make offense a skill" as he moves to redeem time "when men least think I will."

In the "play extempore" when Falstaff and Hal perform a mock version of Hal's forthcoming scene with his father, where he knows he will be chastised for his offensive behavior, the characters take turns playing the two parts. At first Falstaff plays the king and Hal himself, but Falstaff comically turns the conversation from an examination of Hal's vices to a celebration of Falstaff's virtues, so Hal suggests they exchange parts. Now the scene moves from a comically subversive portrait of Hal's relation with his father, to an even darker premonition of the eventual resolution of Hal's relationship with Falstaff. Falstaff (playing Hal) once again finds a way to make himself the subject and culminates his defense of himself by declaring: "Banish plump Jack, and banish all the world." To which the Prince (playing his father) replies: "I do. I will." This is an astonishing moment. How does Hal deliver these four fateful words? Coldly? Quickly? With a wicked smile or a little laugh? How does the actor playing Falstaff respond? Does the threat register? Is there a long pause after "I will" to let the threat hang in the air? Shakespeare doesn't let the moment linger as he immediately has the Sheriff and his "monstrous watch" come knocking at the tavern's door, bringing this little drama to its end.

When in 3.2, Shakespeare gives us the actual confrontation between Hal and his father it is important to note how the two actors react to each other. How does the actor playing Hal respond to his father's harsh tongue-lashing? Is he fully in control of his emotions and assured in his identity? Or is he having to restrain himself from barking back at his father in his own defense? Is he nervous and petulant or calm and collected? What gestures and other examples of body language does he employ to signal his feelings to his father? Conversely, what does the king do when he delivers the lines: "Not an eye/But is a-weary of thy common sight,/Save mine, which hath desired to see thee more…" These nuances of performance are what animate the text and provide each production of the play with its own unique approach to these key relationships in the drama.

1 Henry IV is about the drama of history and Shakespeare exploits the full powers of his dramatic technique to make the play come alive in the theater and in our imaginations. Falstaff is one of Shakespeare's most protean and shape-shifting creations; he emerges from Shakespeare's theatrical imagination, not from the historical record. We need to match our sense of play with his to become swept up in his world, and in the process to discover how remarkably it resonates with our own.

TIMELINE

1364: Birth of Henry Percy (Hotspur)

1367: Birth of the future Richard II (6 January) and Henry IV (3 April)

1376: Death of the Black Prince (Richard's father)

1377: Death of Edward III (Richard's grandfather); accession of Richard II

1381: Peasant's Revolt

1394: Richard in Ireland

1397: Death of Thomas of Woodstock (Richard's uncle)

1399: Death of John of Gaunt; forced abdication of Richard II; Henry IV becomes king.

> This disruption in orderly succession sets the stage for almost 100 years of infighting and civil war among the nobles, all of whom trace their right to the throne back to Richard's grandfather, Edward III.

1400: Earl's Rebellion; death of Richard II

1402: Edmund Mortimer taken prisoner by Owen Glendower; defeat of the Scots at the Battle of Homeldon.

1403: The Battle of Shrewsbury; Hotspur killed.

1405: Rebellion of Archbishop Scrope.

1408: End of the Percy and Glendower opposition to Henry IV.

1413: Death of Henry IV; accession of Henry V

1415: Battle of Agincourt (*Henry V*)

1420: Henry is named heir of France and marries Katherine, daughter of Charles VI (*Henry V*)

> In Shakespeare's version, the French capitulation and marriage of Henry and Katherine appear to follow directly from the battle of Agincourt, but in fact there were five more years of fighting.

1422: Henry V dies prematurely and is succeeded by his nine-month-old son, Henry VI

Because Henry VI is so young, the kingdom is ruled by his uncles and cousins, who cannot agree and fight amongst themselves for personal gain.

Charles IV dies and Henry VI is crowned king of France

Henry V's widow marries Owen Tudor

Their grandson, Henry Tudor, will eventually become king.

1429: Joan of Arc begins freeing France from English control (*1 Henry VI*)

1445: Henry VI marries Margaret of Anjou (*2 Henry VI*)

Henry gives up control of some parts of France as part of the marriage settlement. This unpopular move causes rival factions at court, leading directly to civil war.

1450: By this date, all English-held French territories except the port town of Calais are retaken by the French

1455: First battle of the civil war later dubbed the Wars of the Roses (*3 Henry IV*)

The two sides are the Lancasters (allied with Henry VI and represented by red roses) and the Yorks (allied with the Duke of York, cousin of Henry VI, and represented by white roses)

1461: Edward of York deposes Henry VI and is crowned Edward IV (*3 Henry VI*)

1470: Henry VI is restored briefly to the throne (*3 Henry VI*)

1471: Henry VI is murdered and Edward IV regains the throne (*3 Henry VI*)

1483: Edward IV dies, succeeded by his 12-year-old son, Edward V (*Richard III*)

Richard III takes the throne (*Richard III*)

Edward V and his brother Richard are housed in the Tower of London and never seen again.

In *Richard III*, Richard usurps the throne purely for personal gain, but there is historical evidence that he was motivated by fears of further civil war if a child was crowned.

1485: Battle of Bosworth field, Henry Tudor (son of Edmund Tudor, half brother of Henry VI) defeats Richard III and is crowned Henry VII (*Richard III*)

Henry VII begins the Tudor line and becomes the great grandfather of Elizabeth I, the reigning monarch when Shakespeare composed his history plays.

1513: *The Prince* written by Niccolo Machiavelli: In sixteenth century England, the "Machiavel" was understood as an amoral power seeker who used deceit and violence to succeed. A model for Richard III, and, some critics argue, Henry V.

1564: William Shakespeare born in Stratford-upon-Avon to John and Mary Shakespeare

1567: The opening of the Red Lion Playhouse, the first public playhouse in England.

1582: William Shakespeare marries Anne Hathaway (November)

1583: Birth of Shakespeare's daughter, Susanna (baptised May 26th)

1585: Birth of Shakespeare's son, Hamnet, and daughter, Judith (baptized February 2nd)

1592: Robert Greene's *A Groat's Worth of Wit Bought with a Million of Repentance*, refers to Shakespeare as an "upstart crow."

We do not know exactly when Shakespeare left Stratford for England; the seven years between the birth of the twins and Greene's attack are often called the "lost years." There is much speculation on what Shakespeare did during this time and why he left his wife and children to join the theater in London.

1592-94: Plague years. Theaters closed. Shakespeare wrote his poems and many of his sonnets during this period.

1594: William Shakespeare and Richard Burbage become sharers in the Lord Chamberlain's Men, a company of actors, reorganized when the theaters reopen after the Plague.

Shakespeare would later become a major shareholder in the theater and this, rather than publication of his plays, is how he made his money.

1596: Burial of Hamnet Shakespeare, August 11th, in Stratford.

No record exists of Shakespeare's feelings at the loss of his only son.

1599: Robert Devereux, the Earl of Essex, returns from a failed military campaign in Ireland. The lines of praise in *Henry V* (5.Chorus.30-33) for Essex's assumed triumph date that play to before September 1599.

1603: Death of Elizabeth. James VI of Scotland (b. 1566) crowned King James I of England.

The Lord Chamberlain's Men, recognized as the premier acting troupe in England, become the King's Men. Plays such as *Macbeth* and *The Winter's Tale* are written with King James in mind.

c.1611: Shakespeare retires to Stratford

1616: Death of William Shakespeare (April 23rd).

1623: Publication of the *First Folio*

Without this effort of his friends to collect his works, eighteen of Shakespeare's plays would have been lost.

TOPICS FOR DISCUSSION AND FURTHER STUDY

Critical Issues

1. Historically, Henry IV and Henry Percy (Hotspur) were about the same age. What does Shakespeare gain by making Hotspur much younger and closer in age to Hal, the king's son?

2. Falstaff is Shakespeare's creation; he is not included in the historical material Shakespeare used as a source for his play. What "unofficial" perspectives does Falstaff bring to the play that are created by the imagination of the dramatist rather than the facts of the historian?

3. How do the various strands or threads of the play's plot provide an ironic commentary on one another?

4. Hal boasts that he can "drink with any tinker and in his own language." Find and discuss several examples of Hal's ability to suit his language and rhetoric to those he converses with from Falstaff and Poins to the king and Hotspur? What does this reveal about the prince?

5. Both Hal and Hotspur have fathers and surrogate fathers. What support do those fathers bring to their sons at the Battle of Shrewsbury?

6. Falstaff has been compared with the Lord of Misrule, the figure who presides over Carnival where holiday exuberance and mischief-making trump everyday responsibility and sobriety. Why does Shakespeare plop such a character down in the middle of a serious historical drama where the fate of the nation hangs in the balance? What does he gain by doing so?

7. Examine carefully Hal's eulogies over the fallen bodies of Hotspur and Falstaff. What do they tell us about his relationship to each and about himself?

8. Both Hal and Hotspur use the word "redeem" when talking about something important to each. What does each man wish to "redeem" and what does that tell us about their characters and their fates?

9. Shakespeare finds dramatic power in locating the macrocosm in the microcosm. How does he reflect and perhaps even resolve the crisis in the nation by his handling of the crisis in the king's relationship with his son?

10. For many, Hotspur and Falstaff are the most vital and attractive characters in the drama. What qualities do they share and what issues find them on opposing sides?

Performance Issues

1. If you could direct a film of *1 Henry IV* what contemporary actors would you cast as Hal? Hotspur? Falstaff? Henry IV? Kate? Glendower? Defend your choices.

2. If you were encouraged to set your film in some other historical setting than medieval England, what period and setting would you select and why?

3. What ideas about the character's motivation and psychology would you share with the actor playing Hal in preparation for filming his soliloquy at the end of 1.2? What technical strategies would you employ to make the soliloquy seem more suited to cinematic realization?

4. What ideas would you share with your designer in order to ensure that your film presented a stunning contrast between the scenes set at Henry's court and those at Falstaff's tavern?

5. Orson Welles's treatment of the Battle of Shrewsbury in *Chimes at Midnight* is regarded as one of the great battle scenes in the history of film. What qualities distinguish his treatment of the battle, including the encounter between Hal and Hotspur, and how are they consistent with the tone and atmosphere of his approach to his Shakespearean material?

6. The ESC (English Shakespeare Company) television production of *1 Henry IV* costumes the play, with one key exception, with a variety of twentieth century dress ranging from the Edwardian frock coat worn by the king to Hal's torn jeans. What does the production gain by its 20th century costuming? What does it lose?

7. Productions often associate characters with specific props or gestures which help to define their essence. What specific props or gestures would you suggest to the actors playing Hal, Hotspur, Kate, Falstaff, and the king that might aid them in the realization of their characters?

8. Compare and contrast the great tavern scene (2.4) as it is realized in the BBC and the ESC versions of the play.

BIBLIOGRAPHY

Auden, W.H. "The Prince's Dog" in *The Dyer's Hand*. New York: Random House, 1962, 182-208.

    Auden is one of Falstaff's most perceptive apologists. He sees Falstaff "radiating happiness" as Hal "radiates power."

Barber, C.L. *Shakespeare's Festive Comedy*. Princeton: Princeton University Press, 1959.

    Barber traces the festive, saturnalian pattern at work in Shakespeare's comedies and the impact the tension between holiday and everyday has on form, content, and Falstaff's role in *1 Henry IV*.

Crowl, Samuel. *Shakespeare Observed: Studies in Performance on Stage and Screen*. Athens: Ohio University Press, 1992.

    This volume contains essays on Orson Welles's film *Chimes at Midnight* and the English Shakespeare Company's production of *1 Henry IV* in its epic cycle of Shakespeare's history plays produced under the title: *The Wars of the Roses*.

Greenblatt, Stephen. *Shakespearean Negotiations: The Circulation of Social Energy in Renaissance England*. Berkeley: University of California Press, 1988.

    In his chapter on *1 Henry IV*, "Invisible Bullets," Greenblatt provides a New Historicist reading of the play set in the context of Elizabethan colonial ambitions in the New World.

Greenblatt, Stephen. *Will in the World*. New York: W.W. Norton & Company, 2004.

    Greenblatt's imaginative biography of Shakespeare contains a controversial account of the playwright Robert Greene as a source and model for Shakespeare's creation of Falstaff.

Hapgood, Robert. "*Chimes at Midnight*: from Stage to Screen: The Art of Adaptation." *Shakespeare Survey*, no. 39, 39-52, 1987.

    This essay details Orson Welles's intelligent appropriation of his Shakespearean material both as screenwriter and as film director.

Hodgdon, Barbara. *The End Crowns All*. Princeton: Princeton University Press, 1991.

A provocative analysis of how Shakespeare's concerns in the history plays were embodied and challenged by late twentieth century productions of those plays on stage, film, and television.

Howard, Jean and Rackin, Phyllis. *Engendering a Nation: A Feminist Account of Shakespeare's English Histories*. London and New York: Routledge, 1997.

This study treats *1 and 2 Henry IV* in a single chapter that provides a feminist reading of Mistress Quickly's importance to both plays.

McMillin, Scott. *Shakespeare in Performance: Henry IV, Part One*. Manchester: Manchester University Press, 1991.

The most thorough survey of the play in performance.

Pilkington, Ace. *Screening Shakespeare from Richard II to Henry V*. Newark, DE: University of Delaware Press, 1991.

The only book devoted solely to an examination of film and television productions of the four history plays that compose the second tetralogy.

Rackin, Phyllis. *Stages of History*. Ithaca: Cornell University Press, 1990.

A feminist reading of the relationship between history, drama, and power with an excellent discussion of Falstaff's unique voice and perspective.

Tillyard, E.M.W. *Shakespeare's History Plays*. London: Chatto & Windus, 1944; rep. Penguin, 1962.

Tillyard championed the "Elizabethan world picture" which, he argued, feared chaos and believed in a divinely ordered universe. A classic if conservative reading of Shakespeare's view of history.

Traub, Valerie. *Desire & Anxiety: Circulations of Sexuality in Shakespearean Drama*. London: Routledge, 1992.

Contains a chapter on "Prince Hal's Falstaff" which claims Falstaff for the feminine in body and spirit.

Wilson, John Dover. *The Fortunes of Falstaff*. Cambridge: Cambridge University Press, 1943.

A classic account of Falstaff and his origins in the Braggart Soldier of Roman comedy and the Medieval Vice figure from the Morality Plays tradition.

Filmography

Chimes at Midnight (1966). Dir. Orson Welles. With Orson Welles, John Gielgud, Keith Baxter, Norman Rodway, Margaret Rutherford, Jeanne Moreau. 115 minutes. DVD released in Brazil 2007.

> Welles's film lifts and rearranges Shakespearean material about the Hal-Falstaff story from five plays, primarily *1 and 2 Henry IV*. The film's focus is on Falstaff, from the opening shot of Falstaff and Shallow working their way slowly through a winter landscape, to the film's final frames capturing Falstaff's giant coffin, mounted on a cart, being pushed through the inn yard gates on its way to the grave.

Henry IV, Part One (1979). BBC Television. Dir. David Giles. With David Gwillim, Anthony Quayle, Jon Finch, Tim Piggot-Smith, Brenda Bruce. 170 minutes. The DVD can be bought as part of the BBC *Shakespeare's Histories* Giftbox.

> This production was created specifically for television. Consequently it is shot mostly in medium close-up against the backdrop of studio-created sets which work fine for the court and tavern scenes but leave something to be desired when the play heads to Shrewsbury. The production's values, following the BBC guidelines laid down for the series, are conservative, but David Gwillim creates an engaging Prince Hal and Anthony Quayle is a garrulous Falstaff who directs many of his comic witticisms as asides directly to the camera.

Henry IV, Part One (1989) Dir. Michael Bogdanov. With Michael Pennington, Barry Stanton, Michael Cronin, Andrew Jarvis, June Watson. 172 minutes. DVD release in 2003.

> The English Shakespeare Company's stage performance of the play as recorded for television as part of a seven play cycle of Shakespeare's English Histories presented under the title: *The Wars of the Roses*. This cheeky modern dress production makes a stunning contrast with the BBC version. Bogdanov is determined to present Shakespeare as our

contemporary and the lively production casts a very cynical eye on Hal's rise to power.

My Own Private Idaho (1991). Dir. Gus Van Sant. With River Phoenix, Keanu Reeves, William Reichert, James Russo, Jessie Thomas. 104 minutes. DVD release 2002.

Van Sant's film, in part, retells the Hal-Falstaff story set in Portland, Oregon. The Hal character (Keanu Reeves) is the troubled son of the mayor who hangs around with the leader of the Portland low-life. Van Sant's use of lighting and camera angles in many scenes are a direct homage to Welles's work in *Chimes at Midnight*.